DIGITAL PANDEMIC

Covid-19:
How Tech Went From Bad to Good

Digital Pandemic

Covid-19:
How Tech Went From Bad to Good

Michael Bociurkiw

Digital Pandemic

Covid 19: How Tech Went From Bad to Good

Michael Bociurkiw

Publisher's address and contact information: Michael Bociurkiw, mbociu@gmail.com

Visit our website at DigitalPandemicBook.com
Cataloging-in-Publication Data supplied by:
Library of Congress USA
Library of Congress Control Number: 2021910961
Bociurkiw, Michael, June, 2021
ISBN: 9798726069326

1. Covid-19. 2. Coronavirus. 3. Pandemic. 4. Technology

Printed in the United States of America
Cover illustration by: Antonina Elliott, QuriousWorld, Auckland, New Zealand
Editing by: Nathan Smith, FirstEdit Services, Auckland, New Zealand
Back photo credit: Chrystia Chudczak
Book design by: Jim Bisakowski, BookDesign.ca, Victoria, Canada
First Edition: June 2021
10 9 8 7 6 5 4 3 2 1

For Anastasia (Teta N) who watched over me on earth and now watches from Heaven.

Saluting the late whistleblower, Dr. Li Wenliang of Wuhan, and Chinese citizen journalists Zhang Zhan, Fang Bin, Chen Qiushi and Li Zehua. They paid the ultimate price for daring to speak truth to power.

Contents

Preface. 9

Chapter 1   The Big Read 15

Chapter 2   Wearable Tech: From the Catwalk to Inside
Your Head 33

Chapter 3   Singapore Slings Covid 43

Chapter 4   China's Chornobyl Moment. 57

Chapter 5   Covid-19 Crushes Diplomacy – Just When We
Needed it Most. 69

Chapter 6   Covid-19, Digital Divides, Selfies and
Influencers 81

Chapter 7   Broken News 99

Epilogue. 117

Acknowledgements 123

Notes 126

Preface

A Forest Fire
Looking for Human Wood to Burn

I am often asked why I took such a deep interest in Covid-19. Well, I'd like to meet the person who didn't pay attention to the most important news story of 2020. What a wonderfully serene life that person must live.

I've seen a lot of amazing human events in my time as a journalist and global affairs analyst, but nothing quite like Covid-19. It was scary and destabilising. As the US-based infectious disease expert Michael Osterholm put it to me, the virus was "a forest fire looking for human wood to burn."

The entire point of this book is to highlight how information technology puts us directly beside the grieving mother, amid the chaos of an overwhelmed hospital system, in a cramped apartment, peering over a locked-down city centre or listening to the poetry of an excited scientist. Our smartphone screens are like portals, translocating us from our known living rooms to some unknown vantage to watch almost first-hand a new world-shaking event. Not only was Covid-19 unprecedented in its global scope and damage, but it was also the probably the first truly "global" event we all watched on tiny supercomputers in our back pockets.

The goal of this book – and my job – is to zoom out to 30,000ft for a description of what happened in 2020, the "Year of the New Normal." Viewing the world from such a height can make it look like a confusing palette of colours and blurs. But a journalist's job is to help brush that paint in a way that reveals not just what happened, but what may be coming next.

US journalist Alan Barth once said, news is the "first draft of history." A reporter tries to explain some of the darkest, hopeless corners of the planet. But I prefer to think of my profession as the witness of history. As the chapter "Broken News" in this book suggests, in-person reporting was severely constrained during the pandemic, but by leveraging the wonderful technology of the smartphone, web camera and social media, I and many other journalists managed to stay aloft in the information jet stream.

This book is testament to the modern marvels of silicon chips and LCD screens. It chronicles how the most consequential public health event of our time was used for both good and nefarious purposes by governments, strongmen, corporations and technology companies. The epilogue then offers a series of predictions for how the planet will emerge from the pandemic – including how our relationship with technology will evolve, how global supply chains will change and how we will access healthcare in the future.

Slammed by Covid

March 2021 was the first anniversary of the Covid-19 pandemic. I will never forget the eery feeling of impending doom watching New York, one of the greatest cities on earth, slowly emptying out in advance of the looming lockdowns.

At that time, the real impact of the pandemic was only beginning to come into view and no one knew what to expect. Riding the rails of New York's decrepit subway, it was evident the lockdowns would hurt different kinds of people unevenly, with those on the bottom and the frontline workers (nurses, garbage collectors, store clerks, etc) facing terrible hardship and potentially the loss of their jobs. The lockdowns were initially a good idea, but I also knew millions of people would be unable to stay home, adhere to social distancing rules or home-school their kids. For them, getting outside decided if the family would eat that week. And as new virus variants started ravaging public health systems, prompting yet another wave of punishing lockdowns in the first quarter of 2021, more people were questioning the wisdom of prioritising public health over the economy.

I also noticed how many incredible technology trends were coming of age right as the crisis struck. This book unpacks how the amazing work collaboration tools, tele-health apps, distance learning software and wearable devices were catapulted into the mainstream as humanity searched for ways to cope with an unfamiliar new normal.

This same technology was used by decision-makers in their fretful attempts at "short and sharp" interventions to keep the virus from spreading. Some leaders had more success than others, perhaps due more to geography than the technology. But the myriad devices certainly made their jobs easier. Singapore's no-nonsense, sledgehammer approach to stamping out Covid-19 kept the city-state's case numbers low and its use of technology to get there made it an example for other jurisdictions. Other leaders, like California governor Gavin Newsom, fell afoul of smartphones and social media as citizens used these devices to hold their leaders accountable for travelling while hypocritically pleading with their constituents to stay home.

Overall, the impact of technology during Covid-19 was a bit of a mixed bag. The entire premise of *Digital Crack* – the companion to this book – positions smartphones, social media and Big Tech firmly in the "bad" column. Plenty of experts much smarter than myself worried these new toys were responsible for everything from teenage gaming addiction to relationship breakups. Not to mention all the data they collect and then spin to manipulate us into chasing bottomless time-sinks and going down information rabbit holes.

But the Covid-19 crisis may end up giving technology an image re-boot. The new technology that was previously frowned upon suddenly became indispensable. It let everyone cooped up at home connect with loved ones or consult with health professionals via video chat software such as Zoom. Lockdowns became semi-manageable because we had apps to order takeaway meals or enjoy prosecco-fuelled Happy Hour with friends half a world away. Furthermore, people young and old used the tools to find support groups to cope with loneliness, and the stigmatisation often associated with mental health issues diminished as more admitted to anxiety or depression and openly sought treatment.

The way many people think of technology now is an almost 180 degree turn from what I was hearing just a few months before the pandemic. I recall a rainy morning in 2018 when visiting reSTART, a technology addiction centre near Seattle. Dozens of young gaming addicts told me sad stories of losing almost everything due to their uncontrollable craving for screens. A few months earlier in California's Venice Beach, a born-again app developer called Ramsay Brown passionately explained to me how software developers deliberately code their apps to mess with people's brains in a "weaponised way." He's not entirely wrong. A report released in mid-March 2021, found that 32% of young US adults, especially women and those with lower incomes, reported symptoms of depression because they were unable to detach themselves from their screens.

And speaking of unsavoury forces, the technology did not restrain the bad guys from practicing their craft. For example, while the US was under pressure to clamp down on social media due to a rise in alleged anti-government activity, autocratic nations were finding new ways to use technology to suppress freedom of thought and expression.

To say the Covid-19 pandemic disrupted the plans and dreams of countless individuals is an understatement. The burials of loved ones held in isolation were tragically delayed. Weddings were cancelled or postponed. Exotic trips had to be deferred. Career changes were drastically upended. The stories are endless. As war reporter, writer and Yale Senior Fellow Janine di Giovanni wrote: "Covid-19 brought all our divides painfully to the surface:

who lives, who dies, who gets preferred medical treatment, fresh air, internet for remote learning. Who can pay tuition or afford to flee urban areas for leafy suburbs or the seaside."

Perfectly Imperfect Timing

This book connects the many layers of our inter-connected world. It shows how a small problem simmering in a remote location can explode in no time whatsoever. Covid-19 started as a minor outbreak in Wuhan, China, and morphed into a menace to impact pretty much every person on the planet.

I spent years as staff of and consultant for the United Nations working on the frontlines of public health outbreaks from Pakistan and Nigeria to Colombia and Papua New Guinea. This insider knowledge has informed the chapters of this book and hopefully will help readers understand pandemics. I also drew on insight from my two years with the Organization for Security and Cooperation in Europe (OSCE), the world's largest regional security body.

At the time of writing, this crisis is not yet over. In early May 2021, new variants of the virus are still wreaking havoc and pushing some public health systems to the brink again. Despite the development of several different vaccines, political leaders are pleading for more patience from their exhausted voters. Many of those leaders will no doubt face electoral challenges over their handling of the pandemic as people look for a scapegoat. Some will deserve what's coming. As I wrote for CNN Opinion in March 2021, "if the Covid-19 pandemic response were an exam, many world leaders would have to cheat on their finals to obtain a passing grade."

Ultimately, 2020 proved there are both good and bad aspects of digital technology. Used properly, technology lets people live almost anywhere and still be productive. Technology is lifting millions out of poverty and making new businesses possible in the so-called "gig economy." Smartphones and social media will continue to keep public officials accountable while giving governments an efficient way to send messages to the public on a never-before-seen scale. Digital technology can feel both like an enemy and a lifesaver.

Someone once said writing a book is the loneliest task a person can do. That is doubly true for people writing during a pandemic. But these trials helped me understand the spirit of technological disruption that defines so such much of this present era. I decided from the start to embrace technology and disruption by going digital. The self-publishing route seemed suitable since this book was written mostly in real-time. However, much of the research, I hope, will become part of the archive of the pandemic.

Michael Bociurkiw
May, 2021

CHAPTER 1

The Big Read

An Unexpected Off-Ramp

On the exact second my dusty rental car rolled across the border into Gibraltar, the smartphone buzzed with a new message.

It was 24 January, 2020 and I was on holiday. My relaxed mind dismissed the interruption as just the device automatically switching to a British telecom provider. Perfectly ordinary. Nothing to worry about. The popup didn't even merit a quick glance at the glass screen.

The phone buzzed again. And then again. I rolled my eyes, still exhausted from the previous night's socialising with Spanish friends in Jerez de la Frontera. Maybe I forgot something at their house? If so, I could pick it up later. The vibrating phone could wait until I was done driving for the day.

But four quick notifications later and my holiday mood had evaporated. Whoever was tapping my digital shoulder certainly was persistent. That was an ominous sign. I checked the road for a place to pull over so I could see what all the fuss was about.

The WhatsApp messages were from my former colleague Chris Dobson who was eight time zones away in another old British colony, Hong Kong. Chris was talking about a story that was developing quickly. Apparently, a fresh virus was spiralling out of control on the Chinese mainland. He wanted me to pay attention.

Back when we wrote for rival newspapers on opposite sides of the Hong Kong harbour, I might have ignored this tip. However, I also knew Chris to be a calm and measured journalist so his obvious concern in these messages bothered me.

Conveniently, I had just been asked to write an opinion piece and I was looking for a story. The initial plan was to cover what happened at a recent cabinet retreat when Canadian Prime Minister Justin Trudeau chose to eat pastries from a local shop rather than from an iconic national doughnut chain. A juicy mini scandal, for sure. But an unknown virus in East Asia was a much juicier story.

Chris texted that the central government was shutting down the provincial capital, Wuhan, but there was little clarity on the actual numbers of people infected.

"This is bigger than anything else.

"Get on it!"

I understood why he sounded so concerned. I had seen this all before while working as a journalist in Southeast Asia. In 2003, the region looked on helplessly as SARS infected more than 8000 people, eventually killing 774. But as SARS ravaged Asia's "tiger economies," I also remember the Chinese Communist Party trying to cover up news about the epidemic. Could the CCP be playing the same trick this time? My holiday brain was slowly returning to detective mode as I started the car up again.

A few days after receiving those messages, clear-headed and safely ensconced in a cottage in southern Portugal, I couldn't shake the creeping realisation that this new virus would be much more than a public health emergency localised only to China.

None of the CCP's obsessive and controlling actions since 2003 had changed my mind about what it might do in the event of another pandemic. If anything, the Chinese government was probably much better at hiding the truth today. Whatever was happening in China would soon lead the world into dark times.

Farewell to Business Cards:
A Pandemic of Firsts

Scientists eventually dubbed the new coronavirus "Covid-19," or more technically, SARS-CoV-2. This entirely new form of severe pneumonia marks the first time in modern history all humanity experienced the same invisible menace at once, according to Sony Kapoor, managing director at UK-based think tank Re-Define.

"Every single living human being was affected by Covid-19. Even the world wars were not truly global. Five years from now, you could run into someone at a tiny village in Uruguay or Nepal and instantly connect with them by asking: 'Hey, what did you do during Covid?'" Kapoor said.

While it is true most of the world suffered together – a virus case was even recorded in Antarctica just before Christmas 2020 – a serious technology gap between the many different parts of the world meant villagers in the mountains of Lesotho didn't have the same Covid-19 experience as a London banker or an Uber driver in Miami. The statistics starkly reveal this global disparity.

Consider that about 346 million young people still lack access to the internet today, putting online instruction out of reach of hundreds of millions of students. In Africa alone, three out of five young people are offline, compared to just one in 25 in Europe. Even when they can get internet access, the lucky ones tend to use slow and expensive flip phones which means the digital divide will be yet another obstacle blocking youth in developing nations from leveraging post-Covid opportunities like working from home, telehealth or online shopping.

However, the pandemic has helped shrink this digital gap. According to a joint report by Google, Bain & Company and Temasek, the coronavirus encouraged a "permanent and massive digital adoption spurt" in Southeast Asia in which 40 million people logged onto the internet for the first time in 2020. Much of that region's digital growth also happened in rural areas, where internet penetration was traditionally much lower.

The Covid-19 pandemic struck just as technology became integral to every aspect of our lives. Luckily, this smorgasbord of digital services matured at exactly the right time to let us stay sane while on lockdown for days, weeks or months. While we were twiddling our thumbs, clever apps let us order dinner, consult a doctor or even track a guest's body temperature as they entered our home.

Some of us are now even inserting microchips into our bodies (or placing "wearable" devices on our wrists) to track health data or access homes and cars. And who needs business cards anymore? Now all it takes to swap LinkedIn details at networking events is a touch-less wave of the hand. In the US, people can even access "medical grade Covid-19 screening at scale" with a bio-button which tracks vitals round-the-clock. Singapore went a step further and issued little Bluetooth disks to kids and seniors so they can monitor their exposure to Covid-19.

"Living through a pandemic has not been fun at all, but imagine doing it without this modern technology," said venture capitalist Margit Wennmachers.

I sat down with Bloomberg Television host David Westin on the last day in March 2020 before interviews at the New York City studio were suspended indefinitely. I shared with him my forecast that this pandemic would be an inflection point for technology. Society would be catapulted perhaps a decade into the future by online collaboration tools like Zoom and as a result remote working will be normal. Fitness trackers and smartwatches will make gyms redundant since instructors can just live-stream exercise classes into our living rooms.

Turns out I was mostly correct. Zoom, Skype, Facetime and other instant messaging apps are now deeply ingrained in our daily lives. Abigail Posner, a future-gazer and senior tech executive, agreed that the pandemic has transformed how we live.

"It means we have to do things in our homes that we never really did before – like upgrade our wifi. And it's doable. This is going to impact our ways of working and learning. Just don't forget people still need human interaction," Posner warned.

We had that conversation in early spring 2020. Fast forward a few months and people were blaming Zoom and other apps for relationship breakups. In one humorous episode, a South Korean man was wrongly accused of having an affair with his sister-in-law after an overly aggressive online tracking platform purported to show that they'd dined together. On the extreme end, a prominent US TV legal analyst was fired for pleasuring himself during an online conference call, and Canadian Member of Parliament William Amos was literally caught with his pants down in April 2021 during a streamed House of Commons session, supposedly changing from his jogging kit into business attire. Needless to say, working from home still has a few kinks to iron out (if you'll excuse the pun).

But the overwhelming impact of this new technology was for the good. When international student exchanges were temporarily halted and old folk were locked in their homes for weeks, these two groups connected with an app called Share Ami. Soon, French language students were speaking on video chat with elderly people living in France. Share Ami's founders said the software helps isolated seniors "feel more connected and empowered," adding that the idea became so popular that by December 2020 it had a waiting list of 3600 learners keen to connect with older teachers.

But there was another side to this problem. University students suddenly forced into distance-learning created empty classrooms, shuttered dormitories and cuts to revenue-generating sports teams. This bad situation for universities wasn't entirely the fault of Covid-19, since universities across the world were already struggling with declining enrolment. After all, stratospheric course fees and impossible debt levels were causing hopeful students to second guess going to college well before the outbreak.

"I believe Covid-19 has accelerated challenges and forced us all to think differently – and quickly," Ohio Wesleyan University president Rock Jones told PBS The NewsHour when asked about how the pandemic was affecting universities.

Yet student scepticism has only increased and now a quick search of social media will reveal endless stories of disgruntled students wondering why they still pay normal tuition fees to watch a tenured professor deliver a boring lecture over Zoom. That's a good question for university management teams.

The nexus of technology and Covid-19 also had a major impact on geopolitics. Indeed, the pandemic was the first global emergency in which the US sat on the side-lines as former US president Donald Trump's jaw-dropping abrogation of duty failed to live up to the title of the most powerful nation on earth. The void created by the American retreat meant other aspiring super-powers, such as China, tried to level the technological playing field in its favour.

All this was mostly done without face-to-face negotiations or meetings. With lockdowns and border closures stopping nearly all air travel, diplomacy was crushed. World leaders, diplomats, peacemakers and statesmen were forced to practice their craft online. Although not as much fun as meeting in Paris, Geneva or New York, many seemed to prefer the virtual pow-wows compared with flying across several time zones.

"[The pandemic] has inhibited person-to-person contact and it has certainly inhibited the informality of diplomacy. Virtual diplomacy is still a work in progress – it is not yet the place or the format for trusting and confidential negotiations," International Committee of the Red Cross President Peter Maurer told me in an interview.

The negative aspects of these diplomatic speedbumps became obvious in the first-ever virtual World Health Assembly held by the World Health Organisation (WHO) in May 2020. Live video presentations by officials were scrapped or delayed due to glitches that did little to boost the reputation of the embattled global body. Apparently wizened by the disaster in Geneva, some months later the UN Secretariat in New York asked world leaders to send pre-recorded presentations for its annual General Assembly instead of using Zoom.

Tech Becomes Our Companion

To be sure, the dominance of technology in our lives was rising exponentially each year.

The mini super-computers in our pockets help us navigate, remember birthdays, find facts and complete simple calculations. When a serviceman makes a house call to repair your Tesla car, expect him to show up in a polo shirt and laptop with no wrench in sight. Smartphones are now so powerful that gaming addicts can sneak in a session while sitting in class, at a work meeting or even during a toilet break on date night. Who remembers, in the first weeks of the strict lockdowns in 2020, watching the creative video of someone's hand in a sock "eating" cars as they drive by the window? Or the video from China of people fishing in their home aquarium? Technology entertained us, connected us and gave us a digital chill pill.

Posner, the tech executive, observed back in March 2020 that crises are always the impetus to innovation and to new thinking – and out of sheer necessity.

"Without the normal constraints, humans can come up with new ideas. I am confident and excited about what this will allow us to do in the future," she said.

Governments are also innovating in clever ways by using Bluetooth to track people's contact and movements. Privacy concerns aside (and there are many such concerns), millions happily downloaded apps like this, judging the trade-off was acceptable. Hopefully governments and tech geeks alike will resist any temptation to widen their snooping on our lives once the pandemic is over. But right now, people seem comfortable with the privacy balance of Zoom allowing us to safely talk with our sequestered elder relatives or call the family doctor.

In some ways, this technology made the world much smaller.

But this also presented a new problem: how to find trusted news outlets. In some places, the slow, painful death of local media reversed as people realised they should take more notice of their communities. But this boost did little to help the struggling media sector. The catastrophic impact of years of cutbacks in funding for beat reporting meant few journalists had the skills to cover complex public health matters, let alone follow the day-to-day twists of a global pandemic. Journalists were also using the same internet technology as everyone else to cover all kinds of events. Exotic reporting trips were rare before the pandemic, now they are barely granted at all. The sudden rooted nature of journalism had its own consequences. The Committee to Protect Journalists (CPJ) said nearly every journalist jailed worldwide or shot in 2020 was a local, not a foreign, reporter.

Over on social media, the comfortable careers of pampered influencers disappeared overnight as they lost access to sun-drenched beaches and First-Class plane cabins. Forced like every-one else into lockdowns at home, many lost their only source of income and moved back to their parents' basement. But some influencers were more equal than others.

In October 2020, a few months into the pandemic, celebrity Kim Kardashian West began posting images of her 40th birthday party on a private island. The captions read: "We danced, rode bikes, swam near whales, kayaked, watched a movie on the beach and so much more." Her tone deafness understandably alienated the star's house-bound followers.

The same tone deafness spread among the corporate elite as well. An over-confident cruise ship company, the Norway-based SeaDream Yacht Club, rushed its idle vessels back into service in November 2020 only to summon them back to port after Covid-19 cases appeared onboard a ship. The scenario brought back hor-rific memories of hundreds of sick passengers quarantined off the coast of Japan and the US in the earlier days of the pandemic.

Speaking of rushing things, David Neeleman, the flamboy-ant owner of the US airline Jet Blue, showed surprisingly poor character for such a "cool" brand. In May 2020, it was reported that Neeleman funded a Stanford University study which compared Covid-19 to influenza and showed that the mortality rate didn't justify the lockdowns. The conflict of interest was that the lockdowns had grounded most of his fleet. According to Buzzfeed, the researchers not only received money from the airline mogul, they also consulted with him for their research. Experts have since rejected the study. But it showed how far Neeleman, who also holds a major stake in TAP Air Portugal and Canada's WestJet, was willing to go to push a corporate agenda that may threaten public health.

#WorkFromHome and the Left Behind

The key phenomenon of the pandemic was how quickly technology rammed the workplace into our homes, blurring the line between our professional and personal lives.

Christine Harada, who worked for the Obama administration and was the former chief of staff of the General Services Administration, described it to me as a "great accelerator of the acceptance of people's personal lives outside of work."

And yet bringing technology into the home had a clear downside. Many people I interviewed for this book said they chalked up far more hours than normal by working at home. This often made them feel guilty about eliminating the frontier between the work week and weekends.

Of course, as with any revolution, the introduction of new technology risks leaving some people behind and causing serious social unrest. Back in March at Bloomberg TV studios, I overheard a conversation while in the makeup room between glum staff who had just been told the lockdowns meant there wouldn't be any more work for weeks, possibly months. Those same conversations were surely taking place across the globe.

In an economy driven by skilled workers it was inevitable many would either be fired or furloughed during a pandemic.

Other inequality problems compounded this dynamic. For instance, while frontline workers could keep their jobs, an increasing number of nurses in the US west coast region are African American or Hispanic which the data suggested were at a greater health risk to Covid-19 than folks with European heritage.

This added risk may be why these frontline workers became minor celebrities. Before the pandemic few gave the bin man or the young chap packing our grocery bags a passing glance. But these people were suddenly heroes during the lockdowns for "risking their lives" just doing their jobs. Health workers especially received a lot of praise. They were given daily tributes by the public who would bang kitchen utensils together while standing on their balconies. (It's worth pointing out here that in Brazil, pot banging was how a disgruntled public voiced its displeasure with the government led by its unhinged president, Jair Bolsonaro).

These expressions of gratitude lasted a few months but faded as 2020 ended. One prominent Los Angeles County public health executive, Dr Christina Ghaly, said if the hero-worship was truly genuine, people would have stayed at home to prevent the spread of the virus and help her exhausted medical colleagues.

"Those words ring a little bit hollow. When we see people mingling, or not following public health interventions, it starts to feel discouraging for the healthcare workers putting their lives on the line," she told PBS The NewsHour.

Just weeks into the pandemic plenty of commentary was already highlighting how the pandemic and lockdowns revealed some ugly features about modern society: for instance, the way we care for our seniors, the deplorable state of health among the marginalised and the lack of access to basic health care.

Even in Canada, a member of the G7 club of rich nations, people were shocked to hear how many seniors in some Quebec care homes died of neglect. Those who did survive the lockdown were later found hungry and covered in bedsores and faeces. At least 31 seniors died at a "luxury retirement home" in Montreal. This turned out to be the tip of the iceberg. Countless privately-run care homes across the developed world were shamefully exposed to have similarly horrific incidents, raising serious questions about the ethics of mass warehousing elderly folk.

Woefully unprepared hospitals were also given a well-deserved tongue-lashing by Dr Mike Ryan, the Number Two executive at the WHO. Dr Ryan accused hospitals of operating like low-cost airlines by maximising efficiency and avoiding any real preparation for "mass casualty events" like pandemics. Even the wealthiest societies lacked sufficient hospital beds, personal protective equipment (PPE) and trained healthcare workers.

That prompted plenty of introspection and talk of an urgent need to "build back better" once the virus subsided: "This virus has unmasked the importance of social determinants of health and inequities. We must look at how we can fix these so we can all have the same ability to stay safe," Ontario-based critical care physician Dr Kali Barrett said.

Poor countries with neglected healthcare systems, such as Ukraine or Russia, fared even worse. Despite his bluster about a re-emerging and strong Russia, the pandemic revealed that its president Vladimir Putin had already quietly de-funded the country's hospital network over recent years to help save money. Periodic hospital closures meant healthcare workers had tiny amounts of basic PPE. By summer of 2020, the corpse that was once a functioning health system was so badly dismembered that many staff, unable to protect themselves, were falling sick and some doctors who complained about the situation were mysteriously tumbling out of hospital windows. Dr Anastasia Vasilyeva, who represents a Russian doctors' union, told me Russian hospitals have "become places where you come to die."

But if the public sector was woeful, private companies weren't much better either.

Ignoring all the warning signs, major hotel chains and airlines and so-called "New Economy" brands like TED Talks were all caught flat-footed. Countless firms were forced to pause their operations and furlough employees. Invincible brands at the top of their game were almost overnight brought to their knees, gasping for breath.

Early in the pandemic, before the virus got its name, I watched in agony as Chris Alexander, the celebrity founder of TED talks, tried to keep his company on life support by doing interviews on Zoom from his New York flat. He would occasionally hand the virtual podium to colleagues who had never interviewed before, which led to a lower quality product since they weren't in a room with an audience. Tragically, the total number of views dropped from millions to just a few thousand.

The pandemic changed forever how humans interact, former US Surgeon General Boris Lushniak told me.

"Is the handshake gone for good? I don't know. But the handshake was never a very good public health measure and maybe it is something we need to re-think," he said.

Dr Lushniak is probably correct, but it is hard to see how courtship can be done online. Building a relationship with the Tinder match you found during lockdown can only really work with a face-to-face chat at the local Starbucks. That's something Zoom isn't so good at, yet.

From Flagship to Scrap Heap and Rich to Filthy Rich

Meanwhile, back in the US, deep social inequalities were laid bare.

To use the old cliche, the rich got richer and the poor got poorer. If you were a bartender, influencer, travel writer, event planner, massage therapist, flight attendant, souvenir shop owner, sightseeing guide or personal trainer – then good luck to you. Pilots lost both their jobs and their planes. By late December 2020, many were hanging up their wings – and six-figure salaries – and switching to hourly wage jobs packing shelves or driving trucks. One pilot in Malaysia who was furloughed by Oman Air in July 2020 started up his own burger joint. Another started a food delivery business called Grounded Chef. Alongside them, the Boeing 747 "Queen of the skies" landed in the scrap heap as cash-strapped airlines dumped gas-guzzling jets.

Things weren't much better on the ground, either. Peggy, a long-time bartender in Miami, told me before the pandemic she might haul in US$100,000 in salary and tips in the pulsating bars of South Beach. Fast forward to November 2020 and she was hardly able to make ends meet. Now she might make US$20 a week and sleeps on a friend's sofa. "I wish I was 12 again so I can start over," she grumbled.

While many will certainly find it tough to change careers, plenty of the jobless scientists, ambulance drivers, 911 call centre operators, undertakers, pharmacists, food delivery folks and couriers have shown they worked in careers that were pretty much pandemic-proof.

As in any crisis, some discovered that entrepreneurial blood ran through their veins – and perhaps even a ruthless streak.

One example was Proline Advantage founder Mike Caron, who invented the "Skinny Plate" dieting solution. With no previous experience in procuring healthcare supplies, he managed to land a huge contract from the Canadian government to import masks, gowns and other PPE, valued at a whopping US$290 million. And, get this, his company headquarters is a small home in suburban Ottawa, according to a CBC News investigation. Was this another great example of technology changing everything? Maybe, said Financial Times columnist Henry Mance, but it could be that for the right kind of hustler, "coronavirus has been a rich money-making scheme."

As expected, small businesses everywhere struggled. However, thanks to the massive shift to online shipping, the collective wealth of the richest 651 Americans leaped by more than US$1 trillion to a staggering US$4 trillion, according to the Institute for Policy Studies. The top earners were major supply chain owners (Amazon, FedEx), vaccine manufacturers, healthcare companies and grocery chains. Speaking of Amazon, former CEO Jeff Bezos' personal wealth grew to US$184 billion, an increase of 63%. But that was nothing compared to Dan Gilbert's windfall. The chairman of US mortgage lender Quicken Loans and owner of the Cleveland Cavaliers saw his wealth jump an eye-popping 543% to US$41.8 billion.

Former US President Donald Trump's chief economic adviser and former Chief Operating Officer of Goldman Sachs, Gary Cohn, explained why large companies performed so well during Covid. The Big Box stores and online giants were classified as "essential services" which meant they could stay open during the lockdowns. But the "non-essential" corner shops were decimated and the largest companies "got 100% market share for zero cost," Cohn said.

Yet not every big firm was prepared to meet this new economy. For instance, UK-based Tesco hit the jackpot when the online-enabled grocery chain generated an extra US$1.3 billion in the final quarter of 2020. However, this profit jump was directly proportional to Primark's loss in the same quarter after the latter's brick-and-mortar outlets shut during the lockdowns. France's finance minister Bruno Le Maire called online giants the "only winners" of the Covid crisis and reinvigorated the debate about Amazon's role in the French economy and pressure regulators to break up these online monopolies.

As far back as March, just before the unprecedented New York City shutdown, I warned CNN that folks on the lower economic rungs would find it impossible to stay indoors, avoid crowded places or follow social distancing guidelines. These people couldn't afford Uber rides. I described the frightened faces of minimum wage earners making their last rounds in my hotel overlooking Times Square. I couldn't know then that in the US, between 56 and 74 million at-risk adults lived with or were themselves essential workers, according to the Agency for Healthcare Research and Quality. The Pew Research Centre also found that 76% of low-income workers said their jobs could not be done remotely, compared to 44% of high-income workers.

By May 2021, just as this book was going to print, it was abundantly clear these social divides would be magnified even further with the rushed introduction of digital "vaccine passports" – which required not only access to vaccines but also to modern smartphones. The ability to cross international borders was also dependent on travellers showing proof of a negative Covid-19 test, which can run into the hundreds of US dollars for each test.

Women were hit especially hard by the lockdowns. A new word, "shecession," was coined to describe the massive culling of jobs in the travel, hospitality and service sectors. In the US alone, a quarter of women had to reduce their work hours. By the end of 2020, a whopping two million females had dropped out of the US labour force entirely.

How did this happen? After the 2008 recession, women gravitated to the new "people intensive" travel and lifestyle jobs. But Covid-19 suddenly made those jobs redundant. Many women held onto jobs – both on the frontlines and in the C-suite – but others had to put their careers on hold to mind their children stuck at home. In many cases, not only did their male partner draw a larger paycheque, the kids regarded their mother as the better caregiver! There was one high-profile display of unparalleled chivalry, though. In late 2020, Rubin Ritter, chief executive of Europe's largest online fashion site Zalando, quit his multi-million-euro job to "prioritise" his wife's career.

But it wasn't just the adults that were deeply affected. Kids had already voted with their fingers to snuggle up with their devices and abandon outdoor playgrounds. What only marginally worried parents before the pandemic suddenly became an enormous concern during lockdowns as many children clocked up to seven hours each day in front of a screen. And yet, as soon as spring rolled around, those same kids were clamouring to go back outside but couldn't. Children ended up doing everything at home which placed huge pressure on ill-prepared parents, according to California educator and developer of the Cyber Civics curriculum Diana Graber.

"Kids have to get their schoolwork done on screens. They want to connect with friends on screens. They're bored because everything is closed, so the screens are entertainment. It's more important than ever that we prepare our kids to use technology wisely," Graber said.

Without the technology for e-learning, the lockdown would have been much worse for many families. A Bain & Company report said if not for home-based learning, 135-million school children in Southeast Asia would have lost access to education.

Turning Crisis into Opportunity

As the world economy ground to a halt, those who knew how to pivot had the best chance of survival.

For instance, the Canadian celebrity chef, David Hawksworth, developed new ways of making pizzas and introduced a takeaway option to help save his business. My friend Deisy Suarez-Giles also moved her downtown Los Angeles spa up to the rooftop, complete with curtained-off cabanas and cooling machines. "I was offering sunset and moonlight massages to save my business from total loss. The high temperatures and California wildfires made outdoor treatments during the day almost unbearable." And a woman called Leila in Miami Beach told me she was forced to double her Uber shifts to help feed herself and her kids.

And governments, if they are wise and willing to risk accusations of pork barrel politics, have pledged to dig their economies out of the pandemic while correcting for inequalities and long-standing social gaps. Christine Harada said with the increased awareness and acceptance of people's personal lives, "we are now witnessing more public policy debates and funding allocated to address issues such as support for caregivers and child/elder care." She added that some people on social media are now even calling this kind of support "infrastructure," a view that perhaps would not have been popular without the pandemic.

Emerging from the pandemic stronger than before is a

sensible strategy for individuals, businesses and governments – though doing so will be much tougher for some. Covid-19 is not the first time humans have found a way through a serious crisis. The prudent person will learn from other adaptable people over the course of history.

For instance, after several failed attempts, modern-day explorer Bertrand Piccard successfully circumnavigated the globe twice, first in a hot air balloon in 1999 and then in a solar-powered aircraft in 2016. Piccard's advice for dealing with a crisis is worth repeating.

"An adventure is a crisis that we accept. And a crisis is an adventure that we refuse. That means it's up to us to take the opportunity given to us by the worst disaster.

"Now, there are two ways to move forward. Either we think life is there to destroy us and I will suffer a lot, try nothing new and miss every opportunity. Or I will say: Life is here to challenge me and I will learn something. The goal in a crisis must be to get out of it stronger than we were before. It does not mean richer. It does not mean easy.

"So, ask yourself, what can I learn today? If your restaurant is closed, what should you do? Some people are making a very good business in food delivery by going to the customer instead. Or the taxi driver who has no clients. He can learn a new language to welcome the foreign travellers after the crisis. And he will not just be a taxi driver. He will become a private driver and a guide because he will have more skills.

"Everyone has to find another way to do things because the world has changed. And if we don't change ourselves, we will suffer," Piccard said.

CHAPTER 2

Wearable Tech: From the Catwalk to Inside Your Head

Charmed by Charmed

Katrina Barillova came crashing into my orbit like a blue-eyed fireball.

We literally (and accidentally) bumped into each other at a Singapore technology show in the late 1990s. Tall, statuesque and with killer looks, she stood out from the khaki swarm of trouser-clad geeks milling around the main event hall.

After a few hasty apologies for the collision, Barillova gave me the elevator pitch about her company Charmed Technology and something about "wearable tech." My mind raced thinking about antennae and cocktail dresses but she was referring to internet-connected jewellery. The product in question was called "onHand" – a full feature digital assistant worn on the wrist. Charmed also created convention badges so event delegates like us could automatically exchange business card details when we bumped into each other.

Clearly a brilliant mind, with a background as a spy and then a stint in executive protection, the Czech-born Barillova mistook my nods for an approval and moved on to describe the idea behind her new fashion venture "Brave New Unwired World." Using drop-dead gorgeous models, the catwalk would show off both the beauty and practicality of wearable tech. It was the ultimate marriage of microchips and fashion; of geeks becoming chic. She paused just as the auditorium lights dimmed. Behind me Barillova's models began to strut their stuff, it was hard not to smirk imagining the tolerance of all those khaki trousers in the mostly-male audience quietly being stressed to the max.

Apparently, Charmed was a spin-off company out of the MIT Media Labs. But I could never verify that claim despite my extensive resources as a technology journalist writing for MSNBC and *Forbes* at the time. However, tech start-ups were in vogue during those intoxicating internet-bubble-years just before the new millennium. It wouldn't surprise me if Charmed attracted millions of dollars of seed investment, with minimal sales effort and little due diligence scrutiny. Investors back then, keen to make quick money, probably wouldn't bother questioning why Charmed's products seemed to come from nowhere suddenly market-ready.

The 1990s were heady times indeed. With a business plan scribbled hastily on a cocktail napkin, a confident entrepreneur could land a cool few hundred thousand bucks. Everybody wanted in. And who the hell were we, as cynical technology journalists, to block the popping of celebratory champagne bottles?

Speaking of champagne, at the bubble-fuelled after-party, Barillova, decked out in a chic, designer cocktail dress and with hair cascading down her shoulders, excitedly carried on our earlier conversation about the ambitious growth plans for Charmed. It all seemed so futuristic, especially with my bulky Palm Pilot – precursor to the smartphone – sitting in my pocket. Barillova, in her seductive accent, suggested we meet later in… Silicon Valley for further discussions.

Barillova claimed to have an intriguing life. Before her intelligence days, she briefly worked as a grocery bagger and nanny in rural Oregon then had an epiphany to integrate technology into clothing. She spoke matter-of-factly about how, during Soviet Communism, people had to make their own fashion. "As a young girl, I learned how to sew clothes for myself. Later, when I became an agent, I put different sensors and listening devices into the lining of my own clothes, belts and accessories."

As we unconsciously inched closer, her intoxicating perfume began to work its magic (the phrase "social distancing" wasn't coined yet) and I wondered which three-letter intelligence agency was monitoring our chat through her supposedly secure wearable devices. The Israelis? Russians? Americans? Maybe even the Singaporeans?

Later that evening, with my head luxuriously cradled – not in Barillova's arms but deep in an ostentatious, down-filled Ritz-Carlton Millenia pillow – I reflected on her marketing foreplay. I drifted off to sleep smiling about her high-level corporate seduction.

I never saw the blue-eyed Czech again. Almost two decades later, Barillova, along with her company Charmed Technology, is nowhere to be found – and I mean nowhere. She must have paid a mint to have the internet scrubbed of her digital stiletto prints.

But Barillova was nevertheless prophetic. Wearables, including devices sewn into clothing, have jumped from cocktail napkin to catwalk and now to factory floor.

I was reminded of her in the spring of 2019, two decades after our first meeting. Roaming like a kid in a candy store among stalls at the Wall Street Journal's Future of Everything Festival in lower Manhattan, I noticed that wearables – along with plant-based burgers, delivery start-ups and augmented reality – were now pride of place rather than tucked in the "wacky" corner of the hall. Wearable tech had graduated to the top of the conference speaking agenda.

Barillova, wherever she is, should be pleased her commercial plan for wearables has blossomed into a social good thanks to Covid-19. By mid-2020, plastic Bluetooth-enabled "tokens" were passively monitoring the health of vulnerable seniors and children in Singapore, back where Barillova's models strutted their stuff all those years ago.

Wearables, Hearables, Digestibles

Wearables are now fashionable, produced by big names like the Apple Watch or Google's Fitbit. It seems like every second person has a wearable on their wrist. Online marketplaces also stock smart clothing, smart earwear and even smart eyewear.

Just over a year into the Covid-19 pandemic, multiple companies have already created high-tech gizmos to protect people from the virus – along with devices to ward off boredom while working from home during the lockdowns. At the annual Consumer Electronics Show (CES) – normally held in Las Vegas but in January 2021 was relegated to the virtual – US-based smart tool company Plott unveiled a video doorbell that could measure people's temperature before they are let inside and alerts the homeowner when too many people have entered. Perfect for both germaphobes and anyone looking to avoid a court summons for breaking Covid-19 restrictions.

And for the ultimate geek, it's now possible to buy high-tech masks equipped with a built-in microphone, wireless earbuds, volume controls and a flashlight. Getting a call from the boss while on the go? Saying, "I'm wearing a mask" won't cut it anymore. Other masks have built-in sensors and filters to track a wearer's breathing rate and the outside air-quality index. Without sounding too much like a commercial, these masks are washable and retailing at about US$50 will surely be the ultimate Christmas gift if the pandemic drags into late 2021.

Products like this pushed the wearables market into overdrive in 2020. According to the International Data Corporation, total global shipments in the third quarter of 2020 reached 125 million units, an increase of more than 35% year-on-year. Apple Watch, which introduced the US$200-US$500 wearable device in September 2014, managed to ship a record 11.8 million units in the same quarter – up 75%. Further, Forrester Research predicts smart eyewear may be worn by 14 million US workers by 2025. One of the earliest players in this new category, Spectacles 3 (produced by the makers of Snapchat), is already on the market. The device has two HD cameras and four built-in microphones and can capture 3D photos and videos.

But as cool as these wearables are – especially if they keep people safe from viruses – they do raise legitimate concerns about privacy. Could an over-zealous state use these devices to surreptitiously seize sensitive health information? And, with their inconspicuous design, what prevents an over-sexed 20-year-old wearing Snapchat's Spectacles from filming innocent locker room activity and violating a woman's privacy by uploading the video onto the web?

Moreover, should star athletes worry about their biomarkers being scrutinised in an upcoming contract negotiation? Or might companies be tempted to sell confidential data to a third party without the device owner's consent? The new technology may also prove to be an enormous windfall for extortionists. Criminals could use them to extract money from public figures by holding their stolen data to ransom.

Privacy advocates have already voiced alarm at the potential for devices with facial-recognition software to unwittingly identify strangers walking down the sidewalk. If you think that's far-fetched, think again. It didn't take long after the release of Google Glass in 2014 for an app to be developed called "Winky" which allowed the device to take a photo with the blinking of an eye. Obviously, this raised some significant privacy concerns at the time.

And those concerns haven't gone away during Covid-19. A group of nearly 300 experts has implored companies to respect user privacy in an open letter. "It is vital that, coming out of the current crisis, we do not create a tool that enables large-scale data collection on the population, either now or at a later time," it said. Singaporean officials apparently didn't get the memo. In January 2021, the city-state announced all privacy statements must be revised so any data gathered by its Covid-19 tracking devices can be shared with law enforcement agencies. Clearly there is a two-track view about how much to respect personal privacy during a pandemic.

Privacy advocates aren't the only ones worried about consumer-grade wearables. Everyone from casino-owners, police, psychologists and eye doctors are all nervous as well. Some countries such as Ukraine and Russia are even quickly banning them outright due reasonable to fears about espionage.

Still, the wider rollout of such technology is closer than you think: facial recognition technology is already used widely by police in China and by US law enforcement.

In the Chinese border city of Shenzhen, the hometown of tech giant Huawei, facial recognition technology can identify jaywalkers before they reach the other side of the street, naming and shaming on a large public screen. And in some cities, offenders receive fines for misdemeanours through a text message. Repeat offenders are in for a lot of trouble: the infringement could impact the person's so-called "social credit score" in China making it more difficult for them to apply for jobs or bank loans.

Digital Crack

Unobtrusive, fast and stylish – wearables are the perfect product for the always-on generation. The designers and engineers have cleverly created a ubiquitous experience so users can share photos, check stock prices, swipe on dating apps or read emails.

One of the developers of Apple's iPhone and iPad, Tony Fadell, said people are essentially strapping screens to their wrists. But it's more than that. "Screens are now in front of our eyes all the time for both AR [augmented reality] and VR [virtual reality]. We have tablets, laptops, TVs. It's almost like there are billboards around you all the time. And you can't see clearly the forest through the trees," he said.

Yet it's not all fun and games. These devices are also contributing to a new kind of addiction by enabling round-the-clock, unlimited distractions. For instance, the average adult American picks up their smartphone about 150 times each day. And spending about ten hours each day looking at screens is pretty much the benchmark for adults. Accompanying the gradual blurring of work and home spaces, a new term "technostress" was coined to describe the dangerous overload and stress resulting from using these devices far too much.

But the amount of time the average adult spends online pales in comparison to adolescents: teens now look at their screens so often they essentially live in that utopia of "always on."

California State University Dominguez Hills psychologist Larry Rosen is one of my favourite tech experts. About half a decade ago, his research team noticed how smartphones were suddenly everywhere they looked and wondered how much time people were spending on them. Rosen set up a study about smartphone use among teens and millennials by getting a cohort to install the app Moment (for iPhones) and Instant Quantified Self (for Android). Rosen's team then monitored how many times the participants unlocked their smartphone each day and the number of minutes they spent on their phones.

His findings were gobsmacking. For a start, the gap in between "pickups" is drastically shortening. In 2016, students unlocked their phones 56 times each day for a total of 220 minutes, or about three minutes at a time. A year later, they were unlocking 50 times each day, but for a total of 262 minutes. By 2020, millennials and teens were unlocking their phones more than 70 times a day for 270 minutes.

"We can't seem to keep our faces out of our smartphones for even a minute or two," said Rosen. He added that the ballooning number of available apps is also behind the spike in time spent online. Rosen warns that screens trigger the same pleasure centres in the brain as does pornography, gambling and shopping. The human mind can't resist the lure of screens. To confirm Rosen's findings, just watch your friends reflexively pull out their smartphone every ten minutes or so, as if they are addicted.

Our smartphones have certainly changed our lives for the better, but Rosen's data suggests too much of a good thing can be unhealthy. As Covid-19 arrived, consumer wearables had mostly matured beyond just vanity uses. The devices now do much more than count steps and calorie burn. They can monitor "bio-makers" like heart rate and skin temperature – both indicators of possible viral infection. There's even a wearable device developed by design student Natalie Kerres that mimics fish scales to unobtrusively protect joints from injuries during times of physical exertion.

Manual workers at GM's factories, Amazon warehouses, meat processing plants, found a great use for wearable technology – or "smart PPE." One of the leaders in this sector is Kansas City-based company Kenzen which designs and manufacturers safe PPE for "industrial athletes" working in hot environments or tall structures. But something bigger is happening beneath the surface. For workers who once regarded technology as the enemy eliminating their jobs (through automation and robots), embracing wearables as a way to work more safely may, in the long run, reduce those feelings of alienation that have built up over time, especially in the US.

While younger people more easily adapt to new technologies – especially if it comes with a dopamine rush – those aged 50 years or older need extra convincing, said Kenzen co-founder Heidi Lehmann. Still, there's good reason for them to think wearables won't stop the inevitable tech revolution. In October 2020, the World Economic Forum revealed that job creation is now slowing while job destruction is accelerating. Half of global firms plan to speed up automation in the next five years and 42% expect to reduce their overall workforce. That could mean a whopping 85 million jobs lost across 15 industries in 26 economies.

Factors such as widening inequality, Covid-19 and job losses are compounding together, warned Anti-Defamation League chief executive Jonathan Greenblatt. "We've seen the gap increase between the haves and have-nots. We've seen more and more jobs overseas. We've seen Covid-19 literally demolish communities and cost millions of jobs. This all fits into the narrative about people feeling alienated and afraid," he said.

Researchers will also no doubt set up new studies to assess the impact on children of all that additional screen-time during lockdowns. After being cooped up indoors for so long doing online learning, when the signal comes for a return to normal it will be curious to see if they choose to spend more time outdoors. Will the once-empty playgrounds I saw in every city from Singapore to Kyiv suddenly fill up again? Rosen wasn't so sure. He remained deeply concerned about the long-term impact for kids of near-constant screen time. "I suspect, because of how long this has gone on, that young kids are building habits with screens. And those habits will be hard for them to break. Part of the problem is their parents are also stressed having to work from home when they are not used to that."

Add to this the accumulated stress on teachers and it may be much more difficult for children to break these "bad habits" than Rosen fathoms. Teachers were run off their feet during the lockdowns and many quite rightly complained about the lack of support they received from governments when forced to quickly pivot to online learning. Many teachers simply are not trained in using online technology and it was probably unwise to assume they could figure it all out on their own while juggling the rest of their daily responsibilities. Indeed, of the 3.5 million public school teachers in the US, over one-third said they had considered a career change at least once while working during the pandemic due to the new stresses. It's hard to blame them.

As for manual work, is it doomed? Do people have good reason to fear the "new normal" after the pandemic? Not necessarily, German marketing guru and psychologist Thomas Barta said on a Zoom interview.

"We are at an inflection point of this crisis. The question I ask is: what role can you play? After an initial shock, each crisis opens a window for change. People with ideas and those who can re-shape businesses will be in high demand. If you dare to create the new, then opportunity awaits you in 2021," Barta said.

CHAPTER 3

Singapore Slings Covid

Smooth Operator

S itting down for an interview with Singapore's founding father Lee Kuan Yew was not a job for a timid journalist. Sharp and quick-witted with a breathtaking grasp of history, the late leader had zero bandwidth for fools.

But I interviewed Lee probably more times than any other foreign correspondent, and I gained a deep respect for the affectionately named "old man." At the end of each session, I made a habit of closing the notebook and switching off my tape recorder so we could banter off-the-record about politics – and especially about Malaysia's then-prime minister Mahathir Mohamad. Lee enjoyed hearing all kinds of gossip about his northern neighbour. As we chatted, his civil servant underlings waited outside. It was just me and the commander-in-chief.

Preparation for my annual talks with Lee – hosted in his plush, meticulously-groomed and secure Istana official residence in central Singapore – began weeks before we sat down. All questions had to be submitted to his secretaries so the Cambridge-educated Lee would have notes to use in case he needed them. Of course, the prime minister hardly used these briefs during the interviews, but the formal practice to supply them anyway is a good example of how the managers of the city state behind the scenes leave nothing to chance.

The pre-interview procedure worked a bit like this: I was escorted into a large room next to the prime minister's office where I sometimes waited for an hour while a uniformed guard stood outside, occasionally peeking in to check on me. In those days I hadn't yet discovered the important difference between wearing pure cotton or mixed fabric shirts, so I'd boil away casually fanning at the embarrassing sweat rings formed by what Lee once described as "the enervating climate of equatorial Singapore." But I only felt exhausted after bouncing questions off Lee and parrying his responses. He always maintained a steely gaze, spoke carefully and rarely smiled. I understood his reputation for throwing off the balance of even the most self-assured scribe.

A Fine City in a Rough Neighbourhood

Lee worshipped order and cleanliness, two of the key characteristics that helped Singapore become one of the rare success stories in the terribly unsuccessful year of 2020.

His legacy meant the fine city-state tucked in a rough neighbourhood can still justify maintaining a first-world security apparatus and mandatory conscription. Decades of investment kept Singapore safe from outside attacks on its air-conditioned shopping malls, international airport hub and strategic shipping lanes by its much larger neighbours, Malaysia and Indonesia. But even one of the world's best militaries can do little to defend its citizens from clouds of smog or a newly emerging pandemic.

Air pollution is a real problem for the region. Singapore is hit by an annual blast of haze caused by slash-and-burn clearing of agricultural fields across the Malacca Strait in Indonesia. The smoke billowing from fires burning through tons of carbon-rich peat soil rises into the lower atmosphere and is carried by indiscriminate trade winds to sprinkle over every corner of Singapore. The absolute worst season for this annoying phenomenon was in 2015 when the borderless haze heavily disrupted international air traffic, frightened away tourists and banished the elderly indoors.

It was even blamed for prematurely aging the beautiful skin of Singaporean women.

I was present in Singapore smack dab in the middle of the hazy season one year and casually mentioned to Lee: "Mr. Prime Minister, just so you know, I can smell the smog in the hallways of the Ritz-Carlton Millenia." He seemed surprised and somewhat exasperated. I figured if something could be done to fix this, then Lee would have been the man to do so. But even the best managers cannot control the weather.

When Covid-19 entered Singapore in early 2020, its officials worried the Indonesian government's funds for haze-prevention measures may be diverted to health programmes and thereby exacerbate the annual smog at precisely the worst time. But they needn't have been so concerned. After all, its many years of dealing with bad air and prior pandemics like SARS turned out to be very useful indeed. Since Singaporeans were already comfortable wearing masks, suggesting that they wear them this time to slow down the spread of Covid-19 was easily adopted en masse – without the protests seen in the US or elsewhere. Other East Asian countries with similar history of smog and airborne viruses also had little public pushback against mask mandates.

The question is: why is Singapore still such a smooth operator? Even though Lee is gone, his policy legacy is deeply rooted in the city-state's success, particularly in the tight relationship between the government and the private sector (many of which are state-backed corporations) commonly referred to as "Singapore Inc."

In some ways, it is an almost incestuous relationship, with those on the outside frequently excluded from lucrative contracts and other opportunities. But it is an extremely efficient set up and when it comes to doing things quickly – like distributing vaccines or developing new pandemic-friendly facilities to restart tourism and business – the "Singapore Inc" model works.

This structure served well during the fight against Covid-19 when the city-state brought all business sectors together to combat a common enemy. The World Health Organisation

(WHO) over the course of 2020 frequently singled Singapore out as a shining example of adopting an effective all-of-government, all-of-society approach to solve a pandemic. It was so successful that community organisations and places of worship generally felt comfortable amplifying the government's public health messages from their own platforms. "This is the Singapore spirit at work," observed Singapore Minister for National Development Lawrence Wong.

Also working in Singapore's favour is its small size. The city-state supports only 5.7 million people, most of whom are famously compliant to laws and regulations. It also didn't hurt that the pandemic appeared just as Hong Kongers fleeing unrest in their own city-state started to arrive. They brought with them plenty of money. One Hong Kong tycoon was reported by Reuters to have transferred more than US$100 million to a local Citibank account in 2019. Obviously, Singapore's S$4 trillion (US$2.97 trillion) asset management industry received a nice economic bump at a uniquely tough time.

Indeed, Singapore's geographic position straddling the strategic trade route of the Strait of Malacca makes it a wealthy nation. With these nearly unlimited financial resources – its foreign currency reserve is approximately US$379 billion – the government had enough cash to pay for several rounds of stimulus to keep its citizens afloat. It could also afford a universal free testing programme that resulted in about a fifth of the population being regularly "swabbed" by early November 2020, well before other Western countries could do the same.

Crybabies

Lee had a tough life, but he was not a crybaby. He wrote in his biography how his father would punish bad behaviour by holding him by the ears dangled over the village water well. And his first-hand witness of the "blind and brutal" treatment meted out by Japanese occupying forces in the 1940s would undoubtedly have added several layers to his thick skin.

But those hard times are long gone, and most of the people in his generation are either retired or dead. This circulation of elites has had a profound effect on the mighty city-state. Since Lee's passing in 2015, many Singaporeans are suspicious that their leaders and civil servants may be over-pampered and too soft to confront an increasingly mean, unpredictable and challenging world. Just before he died, Lee also voiced some concern about how many conscripted male citizens were entering military service woefully underprepared. Although it was dismissed at the time, Lee's worry was vindicated in 2017-2019 when four servicemen, including a popular young actor, died during training over a period of 17 months.

Maybe Singapore was a victim of its own wild success? Lee told me in 1995 that he worried Singapore had become "such a cosy place" that managers and workers are happy to stay put.

"We are stuck at home more than any other small nation. A Dutchman doesn't think twice about going to Indonesia or Brazil. But Singaporeans balk at the idea of even going to China in case they miss their creature comforts back home." Lee wanted the younger generations to be trained with a tougher outlook on life so Singaporeans could "get the top jobs when all these [international] companies have branches in the region."

If Lee were around today, he might consider this project to be a failure. The lack of street toughness is now an almost systemic issue. Lee would have been embarrassed in late March 2020 to watch MP Lawrence Wong interrupt his Covid-19 address to Parliament for a sobbing session live on TV.

Wong wasn't the only senior official to cry in public across the world in 2020. He was part of a disturbingly large club. But it is different in a Confucius society since public displays of emotion are frowned upon. Wong's tears generated a good deal of online enmity from the public and the media. "Singapore needs 'strong men and women,' not crybabies who have been pampered by high salaries and ivory towers," screamed a September 2020 headline on the Online Citizen website, as one example. Covid-19 may have exposed some ruffles in modern Singapore, but cataloguing Lee's blind spots would make for a thin list indeed.

Yet during one of our last talks together, I detected some regret about one policy in particular: the speed and forcefulness with which he exported the idea of "Singapore Inc" into the Chinese market in the early 1990s. The idea was simple. In an agreement with China's then-supreme leader Deng Xiaoping, Lee carved out a US$30 billion Singapore-style industrial estate in Suzhou on very attractive terms. China was meant to learn from Singapore's experience while Singaporeans would transfer their "software" and be allowed to set down roots in the fast-growing East Asian economy. (Indeed, the processing time for planning permits was reduced to an astonishing two working days and, during a media visit I saw for myself how expatriate Singaporean managers transformed farmland in this remote part of China into a mini-Singapore).

Even back then, the Chinese were masters at copying ideas and ignoring contract clauses. Before the ink was dry on the joint agreement, China began to build its own estates close to the new Singaporean properties in violation of the exclusivity clause. This led to losses of about US$90 million between 1994 and the end of 2000 and, feeling a bit betrayed, Singaporeans mostly pulled out of the experiment. Eventually Lee's estate started turning a profit – US$71 million in 2003 alone – but China's rejection of his goodwill must have left Lee with a bitter taste in future dealings with the large neighbour.

The misfired experiment in China was mostly an anomaly. But the Singapore's economic model has allowed it to successfully invest in projects around the globe (it was the largest source of foreign investment in Myanmar until the military coup in February 2021). It can also afford to be choosy since it is smaller than Manhattan with four times the island's population. Singapore's isolation also means when chaos appears the borders can be quickly closed, its people closely monitored, the media nudged into line and business facilities shut immediately. During the lifting of one phase of the restrictions, CCTV cameras were placed in clubs and karaoke lounges to monitor the compliance of patrons. The downside of having a tiny section of real estate? Claustrophobia. Despite Lee's laments about his people's waning love of adventure, Singaporeans have developed a bit of a travel bug over the last two decades.

It's easy to see why. Singaporeans are lucky to have some of the world's best beaches and city attractions nearby and easy access to cheap airfares on the world's best airline (Singapore Airlines). That all made getting out of Dodge a common holiday choice. But that was before the tough Covid-19 lockdowns began. It wasn't long before the people accustomed to spur-of-the- moment jaunts to Bali started sharing jokes about feeling "locked-up" rather than "locked-down."

Singapore's borders were so tightly sealed that stranded residents overseas created a Facebook group to trade advice on ways to get back home. And in a quirky twist of fate, well-heeled senior expatriates living in Singapore and elsewhere in the region fled back to their home countries, often before they could even pack up their belongings, since they couldn't go to Bali anymore either. This, in turn, created rare vacancies in the pricey international schools which the stranded Singaporeans snapped up.

As Covid-19 cases eventually dropped, the government tackled the cabin fever by coaxing citizens outside again with discount vouchers for local attractions and restaurants. This was such a "government" thing to do, and it wasn't a silver bullet. Limiting people to local zoos soon wore thin on such a peripatetic people. An expatriate friend told me, "in this small space, how long will it take before everyone has been to the Singapore Flyer or river cruise a hundred times?"

In an attempt to kick-start its ailing tourism sector, the government struck a deal with Hong Kong in November 2020 to create a travel bubble so residents of both locations could travel again. But the idea was quickly scrapped when Hong Kong's

Covid-19 case numbers started climbing later that month, and again in May 2021.

Savvy Planning

It is still too early to judge Singapore's experience with Covid-19. But at this vantage point, it certainly seems like Lee's legacy of a city-state dedicated to meticulous planning and cautiousness was a key factor in its performance in the early days of the pandemic.

For instance, in February 2020, Singapore already had a high-level task force ready to crush the emerging virus. At that time, most Americans didn't even know what a coronavirus was. A total of 200 cases and zero deaths seemed to prove Singapore had great control over the problem and I wrote in March that the US could learn a lot from its strategy.

"Had [the Trump] administration implemented some of the aggressive measures taken by Singapore and Hong Kong, where the outbreak numbers remain relatively low, Americans would likely be in far safer circumstances than they are today," I wrote for CNN.

Using early lockdowns, strict quarantines, testing and contact tracing Singapore set the gold standard for pandemic response. The Singapore strategy was coupled with assurances delivered in flawless English, Mandarin and Malay by prime minister Lee Hsien Loong (Lee's son), that all Covid-related healthcare was to be free of charge.

Another part of its containment strategy was to quickly cut off travel from China – not a painless decision since Chinese nationals make up the largest number of visitors to the city-state. That decision made Singapore, Russia and North Korea the only countries to shutter their borders to the Middle Kingdom at such an early stage. While it wasn't understood then, we now know Singapore's first confirmed case of Covid-19 was a 66-year-old man from Wuhan who arrived on January 20, 2020 – about three weeks after Singapore imposed viral screening. Contact tracing revealed that two Chinese nationals had infected folk at a Singapore church service on January 19, which then spread the virus to a much larger Chinese New Year gathering in the city-state.

But it didn't just block travel, Singapore's government also found new ways to leverage messaging software like WhatsApp to distribute daily updates about case numbers to its citizens. More importantly, the Bluetooth digital contact tracing system TraceTogether, created by Singapore's Government Technology Agency, meant it could speedily identify infected clusters at restaurants, private parties and elsewhere. And it was in near-real time. For instance, anyone could log on and watch the SAFRA Jurong cluster appear in early March which produced "Case 161" – a 71-year-old man who died several weeks later. The technology was supplemented by teams of digital detectives trained in savvy sleuthing and that a vast majority of citizens supported contact tracing.

TraceTogether was ingenious. The data helped pinpoint with astonishing precision where infectious people had visited public places over the last 30 minutes. Maps showed people the exact time an infected person was in a coffee shop so they could determine if they might be infected too. The more people who used the software, the more robust it would become. Data logged any close encounters that may occur over a 21-day period. But the notoriously penny-pinching Singaporeans often declined to use the tracing app because Bluetooth can quickly drain a mobile phone's battery. Thinking quickly of a workaround, the government issued a batch of wearable tokens to do the job (which also made it much easier for tech-less children and the elderly to be traced as well) and the data started flowing again.

Neighbourhood community centres helped to distribute the tokens and officials subtly hinted in the media that if at least 70% of Singaporeans didn't use some version of the technology, the city-state may not relax its lockdown restrictions. A well-informed expatriate said at that point, people were "dying to go back to living," so everyone rushed to get the token. What a great tactic!

Even when government officials admitted in January 2021 that data from the TraceTogether programme may be used in police investigations – reversing an earlier policy guaranteeing some privacy – there was no huge outcry. With its vast CCTV network and government ownership of the largest telco, every adult Singaporean knew they were being watched (some more than others). A few even argued the token brought surveillance more into the open, which could be a good thing.

Once again, Singapore proved its competency. But just like its founder Lee, even the best managers can't plan for everything. Early in the pandemic, the carefully managed Singapore brand took a huge hit. The government was thrown into damage control when a sales conference attended by more than 100 people – including a few from the Covid-19 hotspot Hubei province – spread the virus to at least six Asian and European countries. The oversight caused some countries to issue travel warnings for Singapore.

But the event also jump-started more sophisticated contract tracing practices in Singapore. The government began to incorporate security camera footage, self-reporting forms, travel logs, ride-hailing app records, police tips, airline passenger manifests, international communication channels and the plain old telephone. The new data sources quickly boosted the city-state capabilities to produce Covid-19 activity maps and create savvy sleuthing teams to track down cases.

Nevertheless, the biggest blunder occurred right under officials' noses. Looking back now, I still struggle to explain how it happened.

Sometime in the middle of 2020, a new outbreak spread in the crowded dormitories housing about 323,000 migrant workers from countries like Sri Lanka and Bangladesh. The warning signs existed long before the virus considering tenants often slept several to a room along with eating and shopping together. Singapore's authorities must have known these dormitories had previously experienced outbreaks of dengue fever, Zika virus, measles and tuberculosis. But, for whatever reason, officials ignored the gathering storm clouds. Once the virus got out, Covid-19 cases among the migrant workers predictably surged from an easily-manageable 200 in mid-March 2020, to 24,000 in mid-May 2020 before rising to 54,512 by April 2021.

While the crisis was eventually calmed, some workers and rights groups complained about the punishing quarantines and delay in creating safer living conditions. Prime Minister Lee explained that in the fog of war, "it is not always possible to make perfect decisions."

Low-skilled workers are a bit of a sore point for Singapore. They are considered a needed but unwanted presence by many citizens. Their growing presence over the years attributed to a slip in the polls of the ruling People's Acton Party in the 2011 elections. But as long as manual labour is considered low status in the minds of its citizens, such workers will remain a necessary part of the economy. After travelling through the city-state numerous times, I have heard the phrase: "No one wants to get their hands dirty" on many occasions.

Circuit Breaker

When the new set of Covid-19 case numbers rose too high to stomach in 2020, the government implemented its infamous "circuit-breaker strategy" from April 7 to May 4 and then extended it to June 1. The move was essentially a shutdown of the entire island along with a stay-at-home order and movement restrictions.

This was a big deal for Singaporeans living in cramped public housing complexes, who enjoy dining out. The strategy closed all food establishments, except for takeaway options, drive-thru or deliveries. During one spike of cases in mid-April restrictions were tightened even further. The new rule was that visitor entry into hotspots, starting with popular outdoor markets, would be based on if a person had even or odd numbers of their national ID card number.

Was such a tough response necessary? Did the "circuit-breaker strategy" work? Pretty much. By early 2021, Singapore had one of the lowest total case numbers and deaths per capita – one per 93 people and one per 187,956 people, respectively. That put its results well ahead, by far, of neighbouring Malaysia and Indonesia. By late May 2021, total death numbers were 32 with 61,730 infected since the pandemic began, according to *The New York Times* tracking data.

Sitting down with Bloomberg TV in early March 2020, I pointed to the proactive approach of Singaporean leaders. I explained the city-state's attitude of being "in it for the long run." For example, its government was already preparing for a massive shift to online and remote learning because it understood the education technology trends and acted decisively to get ahead. It had already created an online learning portal for teachers and students called Student Learning Space in 2018, well before Covid-19 struck.

As 2020 ended and while most developed nations were in still various shapes of lockdown, Singapore's preparation and management meant it could cautiously re-open its economy. By late May in 2021, it had already administered 3.4 million doses of the Covid-19 vaccine while 25% of the population had been fully vaccinated.

Now the real work can begin.

Its stabilisation plans included no less than six stimulus packages worth close to S$100 billion (US$74 billion) and a 2021 budget that included another S$11 billion resilience package. Also launched was a bubble near the airport where international business travellers could meet with their Singaporean contacts. The "Connect@Singapore" pilot programme was centred at a high-tech complex capable of hosting 670 guests in 170 meeting rooms. It would employ a "nothing left to chance" model of frequent testing, floor-to-ceiling plexiglass barriers, advanced ventilation systems and tight quarantine areas. However, the still raging pandemic forced the indefinite postponement of the World Economic Forum's Special Annual Meeting along with the high-level Shangri-La Dialogue.

Still, when historians document what happened in 2020, Singapore will be part of an exclusive club of nations which managed to get it mostly right. If success in combatting Covid-19 were an Olympic competition, then Singapore would dominate the podium.

CHAPTER 4

China's Chornobyl Moment

Nuclear Option

The year was 1986. I was working with a group of other reporters in the small newsroom of *The Ukrainian Weekly* in Jersey City when we heard rumours on April 26 about serious trouble at the Chornobyl Nuclear Station 104 kilometres north of the Ukrainian capital Kyiv.

While it is hard for many digital natives alive today to imagine, back in 1986 I couldn't just jump on Twitter to verify the whispers. This was well before the internet and social media and all we had were crackling telephone lines to the Soviet Union. To confirm the stories, journalists started calling up their sources behind the Iron Curtain in a desperate attempt for any possible fragment of information. The rumours sounded bad. We had no idea in those cold April days that Chornobyl would later become the world's worst nuclear disaster and one of the biggest breaking news events of our careers.

The trickling details from Ukraine certainly were dire indeed. An explosion and then a fire had apparently triggered the release of deadly radioactive energy into the heavens at a plant near the border with the Byelorussian SSR (Soviet Socialist Republic). A confused and embarrassed Kremlin hastily set up a news blackout to stop any more information from escaping. But two days after the accident, abnormally high levels of radioactivity were detected more than 1000 kilometres away in Sweden. Soviet authorities were forced to fess up about what really happened. By that time, the newsroom was already hearing of children in Poland receiving iodine to combat the effects of radiation. Yet, confusingly, the May Day parade was still going ahead in Kyiv even as airborne radiation levels surged.

As a small newspaper with limited resources, we did our best to fill the information void by reporting the estimates from sources on both sides of the Iron Curtain that as many as 15,000 people could already be dead from the accident. But the reality was that we could not verify anything. Decades later, it is suggested about 300,000 people were ultimately impacted by the disaster, but no one will ever really know the full tally of human suffering. And all the way until the end of the Cold War, the official Soviet numbers placed the death toll at the absurdly low number of 31.

Recalling those tragic events, former deputy director of the plant Sergei Parashin said it is "hard for the younger generation to imagine that we lived at a time when information was restricted. We didn't have many truths. But this truth was a lie."

Déjà vu

Mark Twain once said history never repeats, but it often rhymes. So it proved thirty years after Chornobyl with the first cases of Covid-19. The whistle-blowers this time were a handful of concerned doctors in Hubei province who noticed an alarming number of patients arriving at their hospitals with pneumonia-like symptoms.

One was Dr. Li Wenliang who messaged his medical school alumni on the popular service WeChat in about December 2019. He said seven of his patients showed signs of a SARS-like illness after visiting a local food market and were presently quarantined in his hospital in Wuhan. Li immediately came under heavy censorship pressure from Chinese authorities to shut down these communications. Weeks later Li was killed by the same virus he was warning about. And the censorship failed, as all censorship inevitably does. As word of a new virus ricocheted across Chinese social media the big cover up went into overdrive to suppress information, punishing or intimidating any enterprising journalist who tried to run the story.

Adopting a "nothing to see here" attitude eerily reminiscent of Soviet authorities after Chornobyl, Chinese officials in Wuhan decided to go ahead with the annual Communist Party meetings and a huge Lunar New Year banquet for more than 10,000 families. To not do so, presumably, would have undermined the government position that everything was fine. Yet both these decisions were likely made knowing full well the city of 11 million was about to enter a hard lockdown and that these gatherings could easily become super spreader events.

Again, similar to the deliberate obfuscation by Soviet officials at Chornobyl, the Chinese government also delayed by about two weeks access for a team of World Health Organisation (WHO) experts tasked with tracing the origin of this rumoured new virus appearing in Wuhan. The WHO team was sent in February 2020, but it wasn't until much later that Beijing confirmed human-to-human transmission for Covid-19 was happening and began sharing crucial data about the virus with the world. Had those WHO experts been allowed to do their jobs, and had the Chinese authorities come clean on the scope of what was unfolding, it might have avoided a lot of damage.

Looking back over 2020, the parallels between the two communist catastrophes keep piling up. But what ultimately made Covid-19 worse than Chornobyl was that humans are now far more interconnected, and radioactivity can't easily be spread by coughing. For instance, Chinese citizens had for years dominated the world's outbound travel market in terms of both numbers and money spent during their trips. This made Chinese tourists the perfect vectors for spreading a novel virus. Yet Beijing's delays and obfuscations resulted in the virus rocketing around the world. By the time this book went to print in May 2021, Covid-19 had sickened over 170 million people, killed more than 3.5 million and caused untold economic damage. The virus was China's "Chornobyl moment."

However, unlike in the diplomatic and public sentiment blowback for the Soviet Union after its disaster, the consequences to China of Covid-19 may ironically not be as bad. In the short-term, the early bungling was a major setback for President Xi Jinping's strategy to paint China as a responsible member of the international community. But perhaps over the longer term, Chinese Communist Party (CCP) leaders may toast to some specific gains from the global disaster. After all, the pandemic offered China a chance to strengthen its ties to friendly nations (or make new friends) by shipping scarce protective gear to their struggling hospitals and life-saving vaccines. China also turned its entire country into a huge lab so it could take the opportunity to get ahead of competitors and test everything from vaccines and stem-cell technology to virtual health software on an unsuspecting population.

Just like the Soviet leaders tried to conceal Chornobyl, the CCP attempted to carry on with its business as usual. It got rid of crucial evidence, detained or imprisoned citizen journalists, scrubbed social media, silenced local officials and engaged in vicious accusatory diplomacy whenever a foreign official dared criticise China in public. The tactic of lumping the blame on everyone else to avoid any awkward questions about what really happened was taken straight from the Soviet playbook. In March 2020, Foreign Ministry spokesperson Zhao Lijian even tried to blame US servicemen for spreading the virus. "Be transparent! Make public your data! US owe us an explanation!" Zhao wrote in a bizarre Twitter thread.

The misinformation campaign was laughable. It made me wonder how today's Russian leadership might react to a new crisis on the magnitude of Chornobyl if it could be transported back in time. While this is impossible to know for sure, one could make an informed guess by how Russian President Vladimir Putin treated lawyer and opposition political leader Alexei Navalny's attempts to expose government corruption. Or perhaps in the way the Kremlin tried to hide the sinking of the nuclear-powered submarine Kursk which exploded in 2000, killing all 119 personnel. If Chornobyl happened at a time with today's computer technology, the Kremlin may have reacted just like the Chinese by arresting prominent opponents, throttling social media and relying on pliant state media outlets to help suppress the truth.

Geopolitical analyst Michael Vatikiotis told me in an interview the instinctive reflex among the Chinese communist regime is always to hide information, while also trying to appear as a responsible member of the international community. He pointed to China's work on creating a Covid-19 vaccine and its desire to share the drug widely even during angry questions about why it covered up the origins of Covid-19. Still, Vatikiotis said, it is precisely this type of authoritarian state centralisation which allowed China to quickly bring the virus under control within its own borders. What other country could force 59 million people into a lengthy lockdown without a sniffle of protest?

It was the very technology Beijing had set up across the country before the pandemic to suppress dissent and law-breakers – surveillance cameras and monitoring software deep in the operating systems of mobile phones – which helped the state manage its lockdowns so effectively. China even used the low-tech but reliable method of pressing into service party-loyal neighbourhood leaders to help snitch on any lockdown violators. Also, Beijing used an existing law requiring a face scan of anyone buying a mobile phone so the state could better monitor each citizen.

In fact, China has an unrivalled network of CCTV cameras dotted across its cities. Some estimates suggest at least 567 million cameras watch Chinese citizens each day - including cameras outside people's front doors and sometimes even inside their house. These electronic eyes, which add up to seven times more surveillance cameras than operating in the US, are a crucial part of a vast national database which assigns "social credit" scores to people based on their conduct and every little interaction with the system. Disloyal citizens can end up on a national blacklist for infractions such as (I'm not making this up) littering, having a messy yard, gossiping or jaywalking.

These surveillance capabilities are a source of pride for China's government and it has already begun to export them to other like-minded nations and leaders. Chinese technicians were reportedly spotted in Myanmar shortly after the February 2021 military coup to bolster the junta's nationwide crackdown. And China's technology has spread so deeply around the world that consumers in some Southeast Asian countries can already go from morning to night exclusively (and often unknowingly) using Chinese-owned companies and technology developed by China.

In other words, the global spurt towards digitisation – accelerated by Covid-19 – may turn out to be of huge benefit to China, particularly as it ramps up exports of technology to a willing international market as the crisis slows down.

Debt Trap and Mask Diplomacy

Well before the pandemic, biopharmaceuticals and medical equipment were considered a priority by the Chinese government in its "Made in China 2025" plan to transform the country into a manufacturing superpower.

By the time 2020 rolled around, the country was a major producer of drugs and essentially the world's warehouse for crucial medical supplies such as masks, ventilators and personal protection equipment (PPE). China's dominance in these sectors created serious supply bottlenecks as the virus spread.

But Beijing was doing more than just controlling biopharmaceuticals. It also kept busy during the pandemic by flexing this soft power. In late 2020, Xi devoted part of his address at the virtual G20 summit to push for a global adoption of China's QR code tracking technology. He said the system would issue health certificates and score people on their potential exposure to Covid-19 using a traffic light code of red, yellow or green.

It is unknown how many bought his offer, but it was not exactly a new approach for China, either. For years, Beijing had leveraged its high-profile Belt and Road Initiative (BRI) project to entice developing countries into what the US called "debt trap diplomacy." Beijing's tactic is to hand out cheap money and offer skills and engineering prowess to build expensive and often unneeded infrastructure in the far corners of the globe. In 2019, I'd seen first-hand how Papua New Guinea, one of the poorest nations on the planet, had signed on for expensive projects ranging from a useless road in Port Moresby to new highways in its remote interior. The bilateral embrace was so tight that Chinese-language direction signs were installed at the capital's airport and hundreds of Chinese workers allowed into remote interior regions. And of course, once these deals are signed, those countries are bound to pay high interest on the loans and back Chinese policies at international fora like the WHO or the United Nations.

The BRI scheme wasn't just about roads and bridges. Using state-linked enterprises like Huawei or ZTE, China tried to reverse its late-comer status after the roll-out of 4G networks by leaping ahead of its competition with 5G networks. To do this, China offered developing nations generous discounts to persuade them into contracting its telecom giants to build the systems. Wall Street analyst Michael Popow told me in an interview that setting global standards with technology like 5G is deeply important for China. However, he believed China has little hope of achieving those policy dreams, especially as the new Biden administration in the US closes ranks with its East Asian allies to offer emerging economies an alternative to China's chequebook dominance.

With indigenisation a top state priority, Chinese technology continues to thrive, especially back home – bolstered by a mix of state subsidies, forced technology transfers, foreign investment and acquisitions. Since most aspects of life in China are already digitalised, and its tech-savvy citizens are often eager to embrace new apps, Covid-19 was a spark to set off a transformation of its health sector. The pandemic meant hospitals and labs were overwhelmed and people began to see hospitals as dangerous. The result was physical visits to hospitals plummeted as people used online platforms instead. There may be no going back with a change this big. China's medical system is in the middle of a huge transformation which will create enormous profit for any early business entrants in this space.

The transformation is also a good example of how opportunity can bloom from crisis. For instance, some Chinese medical professionals felt a burst of innovation and re-purposed some cardiac CTA scan machines to help boost the diagnostic process of looking for lung infections caused by Covid-19. Two firms, DXY and JD Health, also became the poster companies for setting up the new trend of virtual consultations and both reported major revenue gains last year. Boasting 50,000 doctors on the platform dealing with a user base of 20 million, Hangzhou-based DXY is a company to watch. The smart money will follow such savvy companies as they level the playing field of high-quality healthcare for the 800 million internet users in China – the largest online community in the world.

Technology has penetrated much more deeply in China than almost anywhere else. The average Chinese person spends about 28 hours each week online and most already have digital banking and payment apps on their devices. A report by the Boston Consulting Group found 70% of total Chinese mobile internet users (620 million people) accessed online and digital medical services during the pandemic. By 2020, online drug sales in China were forecast to be worth about US$61 billion. Favourable de-regulation is also a major reason online drug sales and virtual consultations exploded over recent years. And with some 130,000 pharmacy chains and several levels of approval and distribution, China now has a real opportunity to shorten its value chain.

Ultimately, the government's goal appears to be to create a closed loop in which patients can consult online with a doctor, receive a prescription, have the drugs delivered and even be reimbursed – all within an ecosystem controlled by an artificial intelligence-enabled audit process to ensure drug provenance and safety. This is an enormously ambitious goal but by March 2021, China had already encountered an odd problem.

Everything seemed to be going well. By early 2021, China was successfully shipping millions of doses of free vaccines to 69 countries – most of them BRI clients – and racing to meet commercial orders from 28 others. Beijing was also offering free vaccines to overseas Chinese citizens and on May 7, 2021, Sinopharm was the first non-Western company to be granted emergency approval by the WHO for its vaccine.

However, very few jabs of Sinovac and state-owned Sinopharm vaccines were ending up in the arms of its own citizens (less than 4% were vaccinated at the time). According to one projection, China would need to cover almost half its population – a whopping 10 million doses each day over seven months – to reach its lofty goal of 40% of citizens, or 560 million, vaccinated by June 2021.

Beijing seemed to make a choice to pursue this "vaccine diplomacy" and side-line its domestic vaccination as part of its wider public relations campaign to dampen criticism of China, showcase Chinese innovation and rehabilitate "China Inc." after the embarrassing flaws in its critical medical goods stockpiles that were exported worldwide. Oxford Analytica senior analyst Benjamin Charlton explained that China "wants to be remembered for its helpfulness rather than its negligence" potentially at the expense of its own citizens. But as of late April 2021, what had been promised greatly exceeded what has been delivered, he said.

By comparison, Russia (which in March 2021 had about the same low vaccination rate as China, or 3.8% of the population) was in a race with China to export its own Sputnik V vaccine. Sputnik V was eventually shipped to about 70 countries (including in some EU member states) and manufactured in multiple regions around the world.

In China's model of vaccine diplomacy, the clear expectation was that recipient countries must guarantee market access to China and adhere to an unwritten set of diplomatic rules of engagement – such as keeping quiet in the UN about China's human rights record (especially in the Xinjiang region), maritime disputes, Taiwan and about Hong Kong. Everyone knows what they need to do.

"It's just naïve to think China and Russia are not using vaccine distribution to garner greater geopolitical advantage," Boston Medical Center Special Pathogens Unit Director Nahid Bhadelia told me.

But many things in life often hide uncontrollable factors – especially among extended global supply chains. According to the Coalition for Epidemic Preparedness Innovations (CEPI), in a normal year some 5.5 billion doses are made, including the seasonal flu vaccine, many of which are manufactured in China. Covid-19 meant another 10-14 billion doses were added to the pile which will only boost China's strength in using vaccine diplomacy to get what it wants. Keep in mind that Beijing also has the added benefit of gathering plenty of data on real-world vaccine results long before Western pharmaceutical firms will.

Chips and Ships

Once the pandemic ends, Beijing's priority is to race ahead with its technology – particularly in biotech, genomics and semiconductor chips.

For that last category, China isn't the only government hoping to become self-sustaining. The semiconductor industry is quickly returning to the days of 1970-80 when every nation saw the chips as critical to their communications and defence. Governments are becoming uneasy considering more than two-thirds of the world's advanced computing chips are made in Taiwan and China still has military designs on one day reclaiming the island. The potential supply chain threat to these chips has not gone unnoticed in the

US. In March 2021, a top US officer told Washington lawmakers that a Chinese takeover of the island was the Pentagon's foremost concern in the Pacific. Geopolitical games are now being played over consumer technology.

Biotech is another potential realm of aggressive economic conflict between China and the US. The concern in Washington is that China will move ahead of its competitors since the Chinese regime is unconstrained by the same ethical issues that slow Western scientific progress. For this reason, stem cell research has boomed in China despite its smaller overall number of specialists. A huge population and lax policies allowing abortion and the isolation of stem cells from aborted fetuses "could together provide fruitful sources for the isolation of human ES cells," wrote Chinese experts in a paper published in Nature. Embryonic stem cells (ES cells) are derived from the inner cell mass of a blastocyst, an early-stage pre-implantation embryo.

The looser consequences of these ethical constraints are not theoretical. In March 2020, Chinese researchers injected more than 100 Covid-19 patients with mesenchymal stem cells (MSCs) derived from human umbilical cords as part of an ongoing trial of prophylactic treatment. In one group of seven patients, all symptoms reportedly disappeared with no side effects. Months later, dozens of trials using MSCs began at Western hospitals, including the University of Miami, with mostly positive results. Although, those experiments were conducted under much tighter regulations than the initial programmes in China.

History will be the judge of China's actions during the Covid-19 crisis. But there is little reason to believe the 100-year-old CCP regime will voluntarily surrender any ground as a rising power – politically, militarily or economically.

Its leadership is increasingly suspicious of any collaboration with the West which does not produce clear win-win dividends. The CCP regime wants to create a more isolationist and aggressive China and to keep all its innovations – even those that could help improve global health – within its own economy. China will continue to use the carrot and stick approach to get ahead. After observing the reactions to Covid-19 around the world and at home, the CCP knows people can be persuaded to give up their rights in exchange for a certain standard of living.

The big question is: How many more pandemics will it take before Western leaders understand China cannot be trusted in maintaining global security, health and order?

CHAPTER 5

Covid-19 Crushes Diplomacy – Just When We Needed it Most

A Perfect Storm

Covid-19 gave everyone a brief window into what might happen if the multilateral structures created after the Second World War were to break down. Few people liked what they saw. And it is mostly technology keeping the fragments from splintering even further apart.

Geopolitical analysts had warned for years about the dangers of weakening the once-unified blocs like the European Union or diplomatic fora like the United Nations. But a deep rot had nevertheless set in and their credibility was in tatters as the vaccines for Covid-19 became ready for distribution in early 2021. Medical scientists and pharmaceutical engineers, who had pooled their research efforts to create the multiple vaccines in record time, watched in disbelief as the "every-man-for-himself" mentality took hold in many capitals around the world. Add to this mix the tiresome habit of national leadership letting political fear dictate their decisions and the sluggish and selfish attitude was painful to witness. And multilateral structures like the World Health Organisation (WHO) were either ignored by leaders or acted so confusingly that they deserved to be ignored. It is difficult to imagine these institutions emerging from this crisis stronger than they went in.

This further weakening of critical global bodies set up precisely to facilitate international cooperation during a crisis will have ripples far beyond the end of the pandemic. Even the venerable United Nations struggled to encourage member-states to listen to WHO protocols on international travel, trade restrictions and warnings against the use of vaccine passports. Journalist and war correspondent Janine di Giovanni believes international organisations proved to be much less effective at keeping the global household in order than almost anyone predicted. Aside from the drop in morale among international diplomats, this realisation will have enormous consequences for peacekeeping as well. In other words, the preventable deaths from Covid-19 may be the least of our worries if global bodies like the UN are no longer seen as credible and cannot mediate simmering conflicts in the world's many hotspots.

Even more glaring was the utter lack of preparedness among wealthier nations for a pandemic, despite many medical practitioners and scientists warning that such a crisis was inevitable. "We have said repeatedly the next pandemic will happen, we just didn't know where or how," New York-based infectious disease epidemiologist Dr. Syra Madad told me.

Even the mighty superpower of the US was caught totally flatfooted. As the global pandemic swept the world, the group of so-called "developed nations" immediately suffered from strained supply chains, an unforgiveable lack of personal protection equipment (PPE) and a medical system that favoured the well-off rather than the most vulnerable. Many hospitals across the Western world discovered they could not handle a mass casualty event, despite some US university hospitals boasting larger budgets than even the WHO, for instance. This realisation may have been the reason some governments were forced to enact unpopular blanket lockdowns after their health officials told them the truth about their nation's woeful pandemic blindspots.

When the after-action reports for Covid-19 are written up for each country, they are likely to include a chronology of how frequent and clear warnings about a potential global pandemic were mostly ignored. One of the foremost voices of concern for years prior to the outbreak was Microsoft founder and philanthropist Bill Gates. He was speaking out about the problem since in 2015 and wrote many articles about it. In one of these warnings, *We're Not Ready for the Next Pandemic*, he described a scientific model that predicted 30 million deaths in one year from a dangerous variant of the common flu. "This could've been worse because the virus could've been more fatal," Gates said about Covid-19 in February 2021.

Zoomed Out

While the world hunkered down, diplomats did not have the same luxury to hang up their lanyards and wait for the crisis to blow over.

During my time with the Organisation for Security and Co-operation in Europe (OSCE) I worked alongside some of these diplomats. My experience of this profession is that it is generally filled with highly-skilled people who can tell you to go to hell in such a way that you actually look forward to the trip. Recall that iconic photo taken at the 2018 G7 summit as world leaders surrounded then-US President Donald Trump to try and bring the narcissistic leader into line. That picture proved that diplomacy is really a contact sport. But with the airplanes grounded and borders sealed tightly, diplomats had a new problem: how to talk to each other securely from halfway across the world? Diplomatic subtleties, flourishes and tricks cannot be performed nearly as well via a Zoom call.

There wasn't much choice. The diplomatic communications had to go virtual if the important discussions were to continue. But talking is only part of a diplomat's job. Being on the ground looking at the realities of a crisis is critical for good diplomacy. Zoom video calls plugged some of the gaps for diplomats yet it also meant many hotspots stopped receiving the velvet glove treatment, and others suddenly were given that treatment. It also raised awkward questions about whether negotiations can be successful if they are done strictly online. No one had ever tried this before and people's lives depended on the results of the impromptu experiment. Diplomats voiced concerns about extending conflicts longer than necessary and contributing to growing distrust between warring parties just because they couldn't be there on the ground.

Yet these were essentially peripheral questions at the top of a large pile of major problems accruing over many years for the fine art of global diplomacy. Even at the best of times diplomatic channels tend to be flimsy and international relationships before Covid-19 had already started to fray.

After decades of multilateral institutions doing the heavy lifting of diplomacy, since the turn of the millennium many capitals had slowly shifted to talk bilaterally instead, bypassing the UN or WHO. Part of the reason this was even possible is the ease of using information technology (especially instantaneous communications like Zoom or email) and the power of modern smartphones.

An extreme example of these two trends merging was Trump's unprecedented use of "tantrum diplomacy" carried out on Twitter without the help of briefings notes or any sensitivity to normal negotiation channels (let alone social norms or intelligence briefings). Trump may not have been especially talented at diplomacy, but he was simply latching on to the wider trend of social media technology to help broadcast his messages unfiltered (Twitter eventually began flagging and then removing any of his tweets that it deemed false, offensive or incited violence, and the social media company suspended his @realDonaldTrump account once his term had ended in 2021).

Long gone are the days when leaders sat in their respective capitals waiting to read foreign news written in long cables sent by trusted envoys stationed in distant embassies. Now a president or prime minister can pick up a smartphone and start talking to a foreign leader immediately. In a world like today's, if a diplomatic action is delayed then the likeliest explanation is political games rather than the slowness of communication. When Petro Poroshenko was elected president of Ukraine in 2014, he waited several agonising months before appointing ambassadors to key capitals in the UK, US, Canada and Australia. Presumably, modern communications technology meant Ukraine could always talk with those countries even if neither had a representative on the ground.

After all, the slow-moving tectonic plates of geopolitics did not hit the pause button as the pandemic raged. Far from it. A glance at the headlines last year will show an exhausting list of cross-border spats, resource arguments, migration patterns and complex negotiations. Diplomats were certainly kept busy on their Zoom calls.

For instance, Armenia and Azerbaijan – with some not-so-quiet interventions from interested third parties like Russia, Israel, Iran and Turkey – picked the middle of a pandemic as a good time to restart their spat for control over the 1700 square-mile enclave of Nagorno-Karabakh. The present iteration of this long-lasting conflict dates to the early 20th century, so there was no way the grievances would be resolved over an internet chat between diplomats. The warring parties eventually agreed to brave Covid-19 and gather in-person in Moscow to hammer out a ceasefire. After three attempts, the fighting finally stopped (but the deep-seated animosity remains), Azerbaijan, with the help of armed drones provided by Turkey, ending up as the victor for this round.

In the September 2020 session of the United Nations General Assembly (UNGA) – the annual Super Bowl of international diplomacy – the meeting was forced to go virtual due to Covid-19 travel restrictions imposed by the New York state. Once again, this denied the diplomats their important face-to-face meetings and the spontaneous hallway talks which are the true secret sauce of getting things done. Even worse, world leaders could not chat to each other in real-time (nor could their entourages go on shopping sprees or perform the diplomatic equivalent of speed dating on the cocktail circuit). They had to submit pre-recorded videos in advance.

The request for recorded video was surely influenced by the disaster at the World Health Assembly – the biggest event on the global health calendar – a few months earlier. In that session, the diplomats tried to accommodate live broadcasts of more than 100 health ministers in what was the equivalent of a technological train wreck. Dozens of video links either could not connect or ministers were cut off mid-sentence. Although the WHO deserves some praise for being the first to experiment with virtual negotiations at a major international summit during a pandemic, it was still an embarrassment for the Geneva-based organisation.

In the run-up to the UNGA, UN Secretary-General António Guterres told journalists that while the 2020 meeting (which coincided with the organisation's 75th anniversary) attracted a record number of delegates, their physical absence was still a disappointment since intractable problems are often only solved when both sides are in the same room. "I still believe personal contact is an essential tool in diplomatic efforts," he said.

That sentiment was echoed by Peter Maurer, the world's top humanitarian diplomat and president of the International Committee of the Red Cross (ICRC). He told me in an interview virtual diplomacy is "still a work in progress and is not yet the place or the format for confidential negotiations." As an example, he pointed to the ICRC-brokered prisoner swap between warring sides in Yemen in the fall of 2020 which used on-the-ground negotiators and online discussions. "An in-person talk is more trustful. You have more flexibility," he explained. Even the OSCE last year was forced to delay a round of talks about the 2008 military conflict in Georgia. "We strongly believe that face-to-face meetings are critical to prevent security incidents and respond to humanitarian needs, especially at a time when there are worrying developments in the region and a surge of the Covid-19 pandemic worldwide."

I can also vouch for the efficacy of face-to-face meetings from my time with the OSCE's Special Monitoring Mission to Ukraine. We were tasked with getting daily access to the crash site of MH17 in mid-2014. This negotiation was done eyeball-to-eyeball sitting across from Russian-backed rebel leaders in a hotel meeting room in Donetsk. The talks often lasted well past midnight as our interlocutors seemed to prefer the cover of darkness to discuss sensitive topics. It's also worth mentioning that they often arrived armed and, late one night, decided to let off a burst of fire into the air just as I was about to go live with CNN's Erin Burnett in New York to report on the day's happenings. Whatever intimidation they were aiming for would not have worked if we were talking on Zoom instead.

Southeast Asia analyst and private diplomat Michael Vatikiotis told me in February 2021 that face-to-face diplomacy will likely remain in limbo for a while yet, at minimum until borders reopen. But the longer this blockage remains, the tougher it will be to return to the status quo ante. "What worries me is the whole architecture of diplomacy has started to show cracks. There is a great danger of a multilateral crisis here. Some countries are simply not talking to each other. It is dangerously breaking down the normal function of diplomacy," Vatikiotis said.

Speaking of mistrust, prominent French political commentator Philippe Moreau Chevrolet told me in March 2021, just after a virtual meeting of EU leaders, that talking on Zoom was creating a secretive atmosphere. He worried that journalists and observers were often being denied access to briefings, view meeting notes and get other official information. "Normally they would be giving material to the press during meetings, lunches and dinner – all of that has disappeared," Moreau Chevrolet said.

Return to Normal Not in Sight

Time is not on the side of international diplomats. The number of active conflict zones – from Yemen and Venezuela to Eastern Ukraine, Myanmar and the Tajikistan-Kyrgyzstan border – are piling higher on their desks.

I doubt any diplomat is happy that under their watch Southeast Asia now has an additional 54 million people living under a military dictatorship after Myanmar's army suddenly cancelled its flourishing democracy. The number of people ruled by a junta in the region now tops 123 million (including Thailand). Often, the generals tended to dump their military fatigues for Versace suits and traded their barracks for gilded palaces. The way I see it, this sort of political camouflage is done not just out of greed, but also to make people forget the brutal methods by which the men seized power.

The 2021 Myanmar coup, for instance, would usually be a priority for diplomats, but it was the colder regional conflicts that kept them up at night in 2020. For instance, a more aggressive China and a distracted US makes the South China Sea, where at least six countries claim overlapping ownership, a major flash point if diplomacy is unsuccessful in keeping the various parties talking at the table. This book is not the right place to unpack all the horrifying consequences if the major global players like China and the US were to start a shooting war. Suffice to say, this would be the last thing a pandemic-ravaged global economy needs.

Diplomacy may have struggled over the last 12 months or so, but the workings of government did not completely shut down during the pandemic. Smooth elections were held in several countries including New Zealand, Bolivia and Israel. The US also managed to limp its way through a strange election at the end of 2020. Though not all elections last year needed to be monitored by impartial observers, Covid-19 was used as an excuse by some leaders to bar outside monitors – for example in, of all places, Trinidad and Tobago. The political opposition in the

Caribbean nation loudly declaimed some last-minute restrictions. Spokespeople for the party were concerned the hasty rules meant the August 2020 general election had "a host of serious irregularities and discrepancies." Despite these concerns, the incumbent party managed to win the election anyway and the opposition has not seriously challenged the victory.

As the crazy year wound-down, civil servants found new ways to cope with the technological changes and European leaders resumed their in-person meetings despite surging case numbers in the bloc. AFP Brussels news editor Dave Clark said the EU leaders felt they "couldn't get their most important agenda items decided because people won't speak frankly when on video." But within days of an in-person, four-day summit in Brussels just before Christmas, the presidents of France and Slovakia both tested positive for Covid-19. It is unclear if they contracted the virus during the summit, but the incident forced the Portuguese prime minister to cancel his three-day tour of Africa in case he too was an asymptomatic carrier. The whole mess sent the bloc back to square one, and as France 24 sarcastically put it about the French President Emmanuel Macron's busy schedule: "Good luck in contact-tracing the 42-year-old workaholic." Understandably, the following EU summit in March 2021 reverted to online once again, much to the chagrin of its leaders.

After watching the weaknesses of the global system over the last 12 months – and seeing the fierce, almost jingoistic, competition to be first in line for vaccines – my hopes are low for a quick restoration of civility in the corridors of power. So too is my confidence in the ability of international bodies like the UN or WHO to orchestrate a coordinated approach to future public health emergencies. Once this is over, I hope the lessons aren't immediately archived to a dingy filing cabinet in the basement under the UN Building in New York.

While the leaders and field staff at the WHO are generally highly competent, their constraints – both when dealing with national health regulations and their own regulations that severely limit their power to call out member states for flouting protocols – leave the world in a very precarious state. In the countries I've worked as a UN staff member or consultant, I've witnessed some ministers of health treating WHO representatives with low respect, almost as veritable secretariats. And as part of UNICEF, I watched with incredulity as country representatives dumbed down situation reports during emergencies to hide the potentially embarrassing actions of host governments. However, the high-handed way in which WHO treated Taiwan – which issued warnings about the coronavirus in December 2019 and managed to contain the virus – was deeply shameful.

It is these sorts of cracks that contributed to the discord and confusion during the pandemic and they will not be papered over so easily after it ends no matter how many time leaders like Canada's Prime Minister Justin Trudeau sing the praises of a "rules-based international order."

This pandemic proved the "international order" is now considered to be little more than a list of rules from which world leaders can cherry pick as they see fit. Global summits meant to bring unanimity have essentially become forums for tantrums. As I wrote for CNN Opinion in June 2019, "whoever screams the loudest or bullies the hardest is permitted to get their way." It is now depressingly normal to read yet another watered-down communique cobbled together to feign consensus after a major summit. At the 2018 Asia-Pacific Economic Cooperation (APEC) meeting in Papua New Guinea, for instance, the delegates managed only to produce an informal summary of pledges, mainly due to pressure from China. Before the end of the meeting, Beijing's negotiators reportedly barged into the office of Foreign Minister Rimbink Pato to "discuss" the wording of the final communique.

Indeed, both China and Russia increasingly see international fora as useless talk shops. Diplomats tell me Russia's president Vladimir Putin isn't interested in being invited back to the G7 club of wealthy nations after getting the boot for the country's illegal occupation of Crimea in 2014.

Both powers are increasingly aligning their conduct using the same playbook of belligerence, aggression and disregard for international norms. By spring of 2021, the Kremlin was busily bullying foreign embassies in Moscow, placing new and draconian restraints on foreign-supported civil society organisations and cracking down on liberal Russian media outlets and foreign journalists.

Perhaps it was naïve to expect humanity to turn a global crisis into an opportunity for mending bridges. A virus was a once-in-a-lifetime chance to unite against a common enemy, to embark on a process of building back better on contentious issues like fighting climate change and bridging the digital divide. That we couldn't cooperate well during this crisis does make me feel a bit pessimistic about humanity's future.

CHAPTER 6

Covid-19, Digital Divides, Selfies and Influencers

A Digital Canyon

Being a young person has never been easy. But future historians might spare a few paragraphs for the unfortunate kids who came of age in 2020 during the Covid-19 pandemic. Those living in low socioeconomic areas had a particularly tough time because their access to technology is still relatively low. For example, research conducted in 2018 showed only half of US households in suburban communities earning under US$30,000 had broadband internet. In 2015, almost five million US households with school-aged children had no broadband, with black and Hispanic houses making up a disproportionate share. Globally, the numbers are even worse – about two thirds of the world's school-age children lack any internet access at home.

Equity has improved since then, but only slowly. Students in poorer families before the pandemic were often relegated to doing their homework at Starbucks cafes – if they even exist in their neighbourhoods – because internet access at home was unaffordable. When this "homework gap" was exacerbated by distance learning some US cities and school districts came up with the ingenious idea to repurpose wifi-enabled school buses as community internet hotspots by parking them in accessible places to offer free connectivity.

Plenty of studies show having slow or zero access to the internet is a major disadvantage to anyone wanting to enrol in online courses, apply for university, write a thesis, bank online, work in the new "gig economy" or even homeschool their children. The problems can get worse as a person enters tertiary education. For many students in non-English speaking countries, the crucial online source material is probably not written in their mother tongue, creating what some experts call a "secondary browsing experience" that can stymie their education.

So, imagine life for a person living in the nexus of these brackets during the lockdowns and school closures. How are they now expected to catch up to their peers?

Those on the luckier side of the social tracks have the opposite problem of too much access to the internet. Many are essentially living in an "always online" reality. While researching the precursor of this book, *Digital Crack*, I visited the playground of the digital glitterati. In Miami Beach just a few weeks before the pandemic turned Florida into one of the most infectious places on earth for Covid-19.

Seeking revelation to better understand the digital divide, my first stop was a New Year's Day mass in a large Spanish-speaking church with many luxury cars parked outside. It was an enjoyable service, but I found it tough to concentrate while a young boy in front of me tapped on his iPad playing video games the entire time – with his parents seemingly oblivious. At some point, his older sister joined in with her iPhone. I'd seen countless children do the same in airport lounges, birthday parties and playgrounds before the pandemic. It was a bit concerning, but no big surprise.

After the service, I strolled to the ultra-hip Standard Hotel on Miami Beach. As I sat at the strategically-positioned outdoor cafe, I watched an immaculately manicured dog take its designer-clad owner for a walk. The dog's owner had one hand on the leash and the other clutching a device. She wandered past a couple from

Taiwan using their device to snap a few selfies in front of the exotic hotel foliage. Behind them I could hear a young lady berate her boyfriend for "scrolling through Instagram instead of talking to me." Later, a handful of yuppie children stepped out of their $469 per night rooms as if in a trance, attached by the eyeballs to their phones. With all this action, I figured this hotel was the epicentre of the fabled "First World problems."

It seemed everyone in Miami was perfectly happy with their technology-mediated lives, but something disturbed me about it all. As day turned to evening and my coffee was replaced by a frosty mojito, I pondered what would happen to their smiles if they were forced by the looming lockdowns to use their smart-phone as the only source of entertainment for weeks on end. If I could track down each of those passers-by today, I would like to know if they've changed their minds about silicon, especially concerning their kids.

Social Media: A Rough Playground

In March 2021, the for-profit organisation, Common Sense Media, confirmed my fears: its survey found that depression rates among young adults and teens had gone through the roof since the pandemic began. Over a third of respondents confessed feeling moderate to severe depression, with many laying the blame directly on a heavier dose of social media.

"Social media can be used for great things, connections and positive impact," said a 20-year-old respondent. "But it can also be used for comparison and self-doubt."

This moral duality was highlighted by the survey which found young people were also using social media to find mental health support. Last year, reports of cyber-bullying and of sexist, racist and homophobic remarks rose in almost direct proportion with the time young people were spending online. It will be intriguing to monitor the scientific research about the ballooning mental health issues for kids. California Health Care Foundation president Sandra Hernandez highlighted the critical need to "stay attuned to young people's mental health needs" when the pandemic ends.

Many experts and studies have indicated that most people look at their phones first thing in the morning and the device is the last thing they see at night, not the person sleeping next to them.

Dan Schawbel, a New York Times best-selling author, agreed such an enormous dopamine rush can hijack anyone's morning routine. They are psychologically being forced to play the comparison game by looking at the highlights of other people's lives. "You willingly start your day on someone else's terms," he explained.

If people are starting their days with such a rush, no wonder they continue checking their phones dozens of times during the day and snapping photos – loads and loads of photos. In 2021, humanity is estimated to capture about 1.4 trillion photos – fuelled by gadgets ranging from smartphones and GoPros to drones, 360° cameras and wearables. That is two magnitudes higher than the measly 380 million photos taken in 2012. This enormous number of digital images works out to an average of 100-200 photos taken per person, per month. Our many different devices and lenses now capture everything from goats and sexy firemen to Starbucks drinks and crazy cats.

"Everybody is taking selfies. Constantly. This must have a psychological effect on our self-esteem, self-worth and identity. You get lost looking for status and wanting everybody to know what you're doing," said Rosina St. James, a victim of cyber-bullying.

This new urge to take selfies has transformed mundane locations into tourist sensations. A favourite example is the toxic lake in Russia's Far East, filled by water waste from a coal-fired plant. Nicknamed "the Siberian Maldives" due to its unnaturally crystal-clear turquoise water, the location often features in the backdrop of selfies taken by thousands of scantily-clad women, newly-weds and others pretending to be somewhere much warmer. The lake even has its own Instagram page. "It looks like I'm in Bali," said blogger Mikhail Onuchin on the caption of one of his posts at the lake.

It's not all fun and games. Status-seekers seem willing to do anything for the perfect selfie and don't seem to care if their actions diminish the cultural importance of a tourist site. Before the pandemic, the Pura Lempuyang Luhur temple in Bali – known as the Gates of Heaven – was a magnet for selfie-lovers and many lined up for hours to take pictures. The attraction wasn't necessarily the temple, but the use of a sneaky mirror under the camera to create an illusion of a reflective lake. This fakery was big business for entrepreneurial locals who began charging handsomely to hold onto the mirrors. A Russian-British woman helped expose the manipulation when she innocuously uploaded a picture of "the man with the mirror" onto her Instagram page, referring to one of the enterprising locals. A commentator under this photo worried the "epidemic of identical photos" set the wrong expectation for visitors to the temple: "There really is nothing more to this experience. And it can come with a two-hour queue time." The builders of such magnificent temples would roll in their graves if they heard their works were now just pretty backdrops for tourists, but that seems to be the case in many places today.

Why do some people want to post selfies doing everyday tasks like drinking coffee? It seems weird to me, but perhaps those pictures are not so bad considering the amount of vile hate that social media seems to attract about so many topics. Abigail Posner, the futurist and tech executive, told me social media is not always such a nasty place. Often, posting selfies in a cafe can be a bit like the act of raising a barn where all the villagers lift up a person's ego and self-worth.

"For example, if I upload a picture of my new haircut, I get a thumbs up, or a thumbs down right away. I am self-making my image through others and I get a sense of how I come across. These positive aspects of social media are under-appreciated," she said.

This feedback loop can actually influence people's thinking, decisions and ideas about what to wear or how to launch a business.

"In essence, I'm building my 'barn' through the help of others, and that 'barn' could be a trip, a book or my thought leadership. I'm literally building my self/future/business through others," Posner said.

Enough is Enough

With so many tourists thronging attractions, some governments were getting fed-up with their self-indulgent behaviour and felt it was time for harsh measures to dissuade the visitors from ruining the special locations.

The city of Rome was applauded for banning people from sitting on the famed Spanish Steps or on edges of the Trevi Fountain in an effort to help "guarantee decorum, security and legality" near the popular sites. A *New York Times* reader commented that when she visited those attractions, about 100 "rude kids" sat on the steps "all on their phones" and were "not exactly polite" when she asked them to move aside. Another reader agreed with Rome's decision since "learning not to desecrate something for the sake of a selfie needs to be taught to each and every person on this planet."

The Italian capital isn't alone in the pushback against inconsiderate influencers and tourists. Indeed, it was with exquisite irony that the first country to slag off influencers is also considered to be the Ground Zero of the perfect selfie – New Zealand.

In a series of advertisements released in January 2021, government-run Tourism New Zealand took a swipe at influencers for their part in stereotyping this natural wonder-filled country. The good-hearted ad depicted a fictional "Social Observation Squad" set up to shame smartphone-toting visitors just before they snap a selfie doing a repetitive pose – such as the "hot tub backshot" or the "summit spread-eagle." "This summer, we're clamping down on anyone travelling under the social influence," the ad said. "Consider this a warning and don't forget to share something new!" At the time of writing, New Zealand was cautiously reopening tourist flights from Australia, but it might be a while before tourism rises back to pre-pandemic levels in the country. Hopefully, when influencers return to New Zealand they will take this advice.

Another tourist location swamped by selfie-lovers was Lake Elsinore in southern California. When an amazing bloom of flame-orange poppies appeared in the nearby Temescal Mountains in the spring of 2019, keen influencers created impossible traffic jams from all directions as they rushed to be the first in the fields. The overwhelmed local government quickly imposed restrictions to limit foot traffic and save the vulnerable flowers from being trampled. The influx of influencers was triggered – not by a media report or ad – but when two people, Jaci Marie Smith and Gulin Cetin (394,000 and 65,000 followers, respectively), posted selfies using the stunning backdrop. Their followers just had to be part of the "new thing."

Down the road in California's Big Sur, which attracts up to seven million tourists annually, officials kept a rap sheet of violations by selfie-takers that might not make a gang member blush, but was certainly a concerning trend. The list ranged from creating traffic, urinating on the historic Highway 1, illegally pitching tents, littering and generally trampling protected vegetation. Local officials worried influencers and selfie-takers were risking their lives and those of others when trying to get the best shot of walking along iconic bridge spans, for instance.

But tighter regulations at tourist sites cannot be blamed on influencers alone. There were simply more tourists in recent years than ever before. Without the pandemic, it was expected in the year of 2020 that the number of world travellers would reach a staggering 1.4 billion, up from about 25 million in 1950. But the 1.4 billion target was reached two years early in 2018, according to data from the UN's World Tourism Organisation.

In 2019, travel contributed a staggering US$9.2 trillion, or 10.4%, to the world's GDP and supported 1 in 10 jobs, according to the World Travel and Tourism Council. The situation was getting out-of-control, so to help bring attention to the problem UK-based activists Responsible Travel created a map of 98 locations in 63 countries which were being "overrun with tourists" or subject to "Disneyfication." Part of the blame must go to the advent of super cheap flights over the last decade, particularly within Europe. "A return flight from the UK to mainland Europe can cost as much as a couple of pizzas and a glass of beer," according to Responsible Travel.

Some people were already burning out from all that selfie-taking. It is not without irony that so many people now feel an urge to unplug and are signing up for short retreats in the same idyllic locations at which they were snapping pics a month prior. Monica Bormetti, who operates Smartbreak "digital detox" retreats in Milan and is author of the book #EGOPHONIA, said the people "need to find ways to balance the use of technology to avoid the risk of being overwhelmed." Her retreat attracts burned-out folk who generally fall into three categories: 1) those who want a break but can't imagine going a whole day without an internet connection; 2) people who can unplug and describe their day off as almost a holiday; and 3) a large group who try to relax but feel a bit bored and unconsciously keep looking for their phone. Bormetti isn't optimistic about the speed of change regarding how much time people should spend with screens. "Today the norm is to scroll on a screen, not to hold a crayon," she said.

Bormetti's concerns were often intended by the very creators of the devices. It's no secret that, given the addictive powers of digital devices, many are now advocating for more balance. Imran Chaudhri, the iPhone's original user-interface designer, told me that could involve "a drastic shift in the way people interact with technology."

This is a problem because, when it comes to children, devices can be like a digital drug. My friend Elspeth Day is the mother of a five-year-old and an eight-year-old. The older child can easily detach herself from the iPad, but "those screens are 100% heroin for young kids," she wrote to me in an email exchange.

"After any iPad use, it takes about four days for withdrawal to end. They complain incessantly, can't think of anything else, won't be rambunctious, won't play with their toys, won't draw, won't read. When still in device mode, in short, they have tantrums about anything - bed time, bath time, etc.

"But once they forget that iPads exist, they go back to being lovely children. I'm tempted to get rid of the devices entirely," Day said.

The best advice I have is to monitor what children do on the screens rather than how much time they spend on them. And the more frequently parents can schedule "no-device" family time, the better.

Covid-19 vs The World's Newest Job

Yet there are plenty of people with the Orwellian job title of "influencer" who have discovered intriguing ways to be paid for their social media use. They take selfies for a living.

As the pandemic forced everyone to re-evaluate their lives, the social media influencers were hit particularly hard, and the profession faced an existential crisis. They either fell out of favour, changed how they operated – hardly one to skip a beat, actress and L'Oréal brand ambassador Eva Longoria filmed herself dying her greying hair at home under lockdown for an audience of roughly eight million – or used their skills for altruistic reasons like charity work and partnering with online mental health providers. They really had no other choice. Not only were people barred from travelling due to lockdowns, as the vaccines emerged the wider travel industry announced dramatic changes that would alter the livelihoods for influencers.

Thinking about this, I realised my trip to Miami Beach may have unknowingly witnessed the passing parade of history. All those influencers and smartphone-obsessed people packed into resorts, airlines and cruise ships taking picture-perfect, filtered photos. Would they return after Covid-19? What would happen to the business models of social media companies if fewer people were out there keeping the pipelines moving with fresh social media content? The sector had become so nuanced that to become an influencer, you could fit into one of many tiers. One could be a "nano-influencer" (500-5000 followers), "micro-influencer" (5000-30,000), "celebrity influencer," "power influencer," "gaming influencer" or even "kidfluencer." But there were never enough people to do these strange new jobs. In response, some larger companies developed their own computer-generated influencers to both save money and ensure their marketing message is delivered correctly.

If you can get the gig, being an influencer can be a lucrative job. A 2020 survey by social intelligence platform Klear of more than 4800 influencers showed that, on average, influencers earn between US$65 to US$4678 per social media post – with videos clocking in at the upper end of the pay scale. Surprisingly, considering that women make up 84% of all influencers, male influencers still tend to earn at the upper end of that pay scale. Indeed, the Klear survey found women earn on average US$128 less per post than male influencers, with the highest pay gap occurring on YouTube. Of course, the job of influencing is much wider than just travel, but in the travel sector alone, the pay gap unsurprisingly goes in the other direction with women making about on average US$45 more per post than men.

That disparity may be due to the other, unspoken gap between the sexes. Not only are female influencers expected to settle for less pay, they are also encouraged to integrate a "heavy dose of sex appeal" – as close to nude as possible – into every picture, post and video, according to the personal experience of visual artist and former influencer Ciara Kleva. "Men can stand next to a BMW with the hashtag #motivation, but I was asked to bend over next to a tub of protein and hashtag #inspiration. This is what we're dealing with now," said Kleva.

The new influencer sector is much younger than most of its practitioners (Instagram was launched in 2010). But in that short window of time, influencers of all stripes have played a major role in the last decade's travel sector boom. The sector, when measured against international tourist arrivals, expanded by almost 4% in 2019. Obviously, social media had something to do with the rise and rise of travel as a hobby. And even in the middle of a pandemic, analysts still expect the sector to only slow down in 2021, not come to a complete halt. Many brands, responding to data showing people spent more time on social media during the pandemic, now plan to nearly double their spending on influencer marketing to a staggering US$15 billion by 2022, according to a report by Insider Intelligence.

After all, even if people can't fly, they can still buy – everything from luggage and clothing to booking future stays at resorts or on adventure vacations. According to one industry insider, the brands are trying to capitalise on the "anti-travel travel" movement that sprung up as a reaction to the pandemic. Marketers have their hands on statistics showing what people are spending money on today, and what that they've saved by not commuting, travelling or enjoying outdoor entertainment during the pandemic.

As 2020 turned into 2021, the influencers sector was radically changed. Brands now focus much more on Gen Z (aged 18-24) partners and are creating new sponsored collaborations. Many brands are even becoming social activists themselves. The so-called "aspirational" glamourous content did not completely fade away but took on a more socially-responsible tone, though in many cases with only the thinnest of genuine veneer.

As one can imagine, the glamour of social media attracted millions of people to pick up the job of influencer. For a while, the rumours of high-paying gigs, free travel and the chance to hobnob with stars created a feeding frenzy. In turn, real talent gravitated to the profession and it began to mature. But by about 2019, many brands sensed they were getting little "ROI" or bang for their buck and started demanding aspiring new influencers prove they had real accounts and hadn't purchased fake "followers" to artificially boost their popularity. One way companies weeded out the talented candidates was to calculate how many engagements the influencer had with the audience, along with the depth and meaningfulness of that contact. It was a rough guesstimate, but it helped, according to Ralf Tesch of Germany-based travel and lifestyle brand @LoveLifePassport, who said a high number of followers "doesn't necessarily mean a person actually has any influence."

Other, more official, tweaks to the Wild West of influencing have been developed by the owners of the social media sites themselves. For instance, starting in 2017, Instagram (owned by Facebook) introduced a new paid partnership feature allowing influencers to tag all the posts which are sponsored. A bit like a warning label for product placement. Don't misread this: it's not as if Instagram executives had an epiphany and decided to stand on the moral high ground. They made this change as a response to pressure from the US Federal Trade Commission (FTC) for social media companies to more closely align with the government's guidelines for marketing endorsements. The FTC wants the companies to do even more since the new sponsorship labels are difficult to spot and it's not always clear what they mean.

For instance, travel influencers like Scott and Collette Stohler (@roamaroo with 238,000 followers) pivoted early in the pandemic towards "socially distanced travel" and moved into an Airstream Inc. travel trailer. However, none of their posts on Instagram appear to be labelled as a "paid partnership" with Airstream, even though the company confirmed to me the couple are "brand ambassadors." (An Airstream spokesperson refused to comment on why the FTC labels were not being used in the Stohler's posts).

Still, the greater the transparency, the greater chance the social media ecosystem has of surviving intact after the pandemic. The biggest attraction of social media is the ability for people to share the exciting times of their lives. It is understandable that companies and influencers have to pay their bills, but shoving corporate marketing into the middle of a video reel about the birth of a nephew risks turning people off the technology. A new balance will be needed.

Then again, the point is moot until influencers can start travelling once more. While awaiting the resumption of flights, and to keep her channel humming, Instagram influencer Selena Taylor of Amsterdam (@finduslost – 170K followers) managed to keep her paid partnerships with the Crabtree & Evelyn brand by re-purposing content from earlier trips. By late April 2021, her follower count had only dipped by 3000 people, and she even launched an online shop to sell prints of her photos from past trips. Taylor was mostly honest about her tactic of re-packaging already-posted material due to being stuck at home. But other influencers still wanted to project themselves as jet-setters, even if they couldn't travel outside their country's borders.

In normal times, the day job of Eric Stoen is to travel the world with his wife and three children. While it seems strange to say so, he has become so good at this job that he is "the world's #4 most influential traveller," according to his Instagram bio. During the Covid-19 pandemic, Stoen's international travel days were temporarily over so he turned the smartphone camera lens to capture national parks in the US, in the process increasing his followers. Another influencer Callum Snape (@calsnape – 815,000 followers) adapted in a similar way by stepping outside to film nearby locations in his hometown of Vancouver and beyond. He has managed to hold onto most of his followers.

"A lot of tone-deaf influencers are promoting places like Tahiti and Mexico," Snape wrote to me in an email conversation. "Some are being held accountable for their actions by peers and their audience. The pandemic is forcing some people into making tricky moral decisions to financially survive, especially if a company approaches them with a paid gig and they don't live somewhere with the same social welfare aid for out-of-work professionals as in Canada," he said.

Big changes have clearly hit the world's newest job, and even bigger changes are likely coming. The million-dollar question is:

will all that reflective time spent in lockdowns change influencer attitudes for the better? Snape thinks it will. In fact, he already sees clients acting more selective about which influencers they hire and searching for people with "good moral compasses," he said.

Rules for Thee But Not for Me

An attitude shift is certainly needed among the elected politicians, officials and celebrities using these platforms.

Early in the pandemic, I started documenting examples of the tone-deafness Callum Snape described as some people were caught flouting lockdown rules and breaking pandemic etiquette. The worst offenders were elected politicians. I noted many leaders playing fast and loose with the facts, manipulating their own words, and then embarrassingly begging for voters' forgiveness. One egregious example was a Canadian politician, Ontario minister of finance Rod Phillips, who recorded a 2020 Christmas message urging people to "stay at home" and then flew off to get a sun tan on a foreign beach (he was later forced to resign). Shachi Kurl, president of the Angus Reid Institute, a Canadian polling organisation, said such hypocrisy ruined the esprit de corps built over weeks of tough lockdowns and brought to mind the saying: "Rules for thee, but not for me."

My journalism skills were not required to uncover incidents like this. All I needed to do was open up the homepages of social media and I was inundated with images of important people who couldn't resist posting pictures of themselves lying on sun-drenched beaches, enjoying off-limit ski pistes or attending distant conferences.

But the Bad-Etiquette Award should go to TV star Kim Kardashian. In October 2020, in the middle of the pandemic that had already killed a quarter-of-a-million of her fellow Americans, Kardashian flew 40 of her closest friends and family on a char-tered Boeing-777 to a birthday bash on a remote tropical island.

In a post afterwards to her 70 million Twitter followers, the celebrity influencer spoke of kayaking, whale watching, bike riding and movies on the beach. "40 and feeling so humbled and blessed," she tweeted.

The backlash was immediate – and loud. Hundreds of thousands of stunned Twitter followers decried her tone deafness. One account said, "whatever possessed Kim Kardashian to make an entire thread about her lavish birthday trip that, with or without a pandemic 99.9% of people can't afford, is beyond me." Rock legend Peter Frampton joined the condemnation by tweeting: "Are you that insensitive? People are going to food banks not private islands!"

It wasn't a one-off situation, either. The bad etiquette kept happening. In November 2020, just as most Canadians were under lockdown or stuck at home heeding advice not to travel, Vancouver-based life coach Leah Brathwaite made a dash for the surf and sun of Hawaii. The self-proclaimed micro-influencer, said she felt "called" to the islands and her explanation after being ferociously attacked online was bizarre:

"Why? I wasn't entirely sure. But there's something special about Maui that reconnects me to my heart and every time I go, I come back changed. This trip I learned to accept myself and others with less judgement. I connected with people I love. I met the sweetest stripper and had lunch with a gentle soul who had killed a man. I saw whales and rainbows and cried at the top of a volcano."

This kind of foul behaviour has unfortunately continued into 2021. Just as an Arctic chill shut down Texas in February, plunging millions into darkness, Senator Ted Cruz (R-TX) boarded a plane with his family for the beaches of Cancun. The prospective 2024 presidential contender said his family vacation was "obviously a mistake" and that he started to second-guess the trip the moment he boarded the plane (or probably more accurately when he realised fellow passengers were snapping photos of him for their own social media). Cruz, a master of language due to his legal training, tried to wiggle out of the predicament by saying he succumbed to pressure from his kids to bail on sub-zero temperatures in Texas to get them some sun. After *The New York Times* revealed Cruz's wife Heather sent group text messages to invite their neighbours to the sojourn, the Senator sheepishly changed his story.

The lesson of these stories? When your job is to get people to watch you, they will watch you all the time. The increased social media scrutiny seemed to catch everyone in the same net of public disapproval. Canadian commentator Cathal Kelly described influencers as people who turned "tedium into a business" and whose currency is attention.

"This art form creates no joy, neither in the creation nor the consumption of it. It makes everyone who encounters it feel worse about themselves. It is insidious because it creates the illusion of human connection, but without any of the intimacy that defines actual friendship. It is the equivalent of feeling part of the great flow of humanity by riding the subway alone during rush hour. Only worse," he wrote.

Perhaps this was an over-reaction, but it was directionally accurate. New York-based psychiatrist Sue Varma helped explain the tone-deafness of celebrities and politicians. She told me in an interview such folk often feel like the rules don't apply to them.

"With power, we sometimes see people display less empathy. And the reason we turn to influencers is because it fulfils our voyeurism and escapism. Yet on some level, we also wish to relate to them. This becomes difficult during a crisis when their projected lives are in stark contrast to how we might be experiencing the world.

"Most people, including influencers, want to be able to live life without public scrutiny, but where there is visibility, there is scrutiny. And for most influencers, keeping the public hooked leads to more engagement which translates into potential endorsements. And I mean, if a tree falls in a forest and you did not Instagram it, did it really happen?" Varma said.

Even corporations were caught crossing ethical red lines

during the pandemic. In October 2020, word leaked out that Hong Kong's low-cost airline, HK Express, was planning to transport a group of influencers on a 90-minute "flight to nowhere" during a week that the city was placed in lockdown. Angry critics said the airline was gratuitously contributing to global warming and sending the wrong signal when other carriers were forced to enact deep job cuts. In a tone-deaf response, HK Express told the *South China Morning Post* the flight was to help people "rediscover the joy of flying."

Air Canada also leveraged influencers to encourage travel at the same time the Canadian government begged its citizens to stay home. A sponsored trip to Jamaica in November 2020 resulted a senior Canadian government official leaving her post. She became, you guessed it, a full-time influencer.

Social Audio: Passing Fad or Here to Stay?

When living in London as a boy, my parents dragged us into the city for post-church Sunday visits to Hyde Park. In one outing, we visited the northeast corner and the famed Speakers' Corner.

In existence since the mid-1800s, the location is a soapbox where anyone can show up unannounced and give forth on political and social topics of the day. Figures from George Orwell, Vladimir Lenin and Karl Marx all reportedly tried to convert the masses from this outdoor free-speech bastion. Orwell described Speakers' Corner as "one of the minor wonders of the world" where he heard Indian nationalists, temperance reformers, Communists, Trotskyists, the Socialist Party of Great Britain, the Catholic Evidence Society, freethinkers, vegetarians, Mormons, the Salvation Army, the Church Army and "a large variety of plain lunatics." Clutching my mother's hand, unable to comprehend what was being said, the loud voices and energy on that day were something I recall clearly to this day.

During the pandemic, Speaker's Corner was deserted for many months. But political discussion in public has never been more common. In a way, the new Speaker's Corner is the many virtual speaking platforms. People gravitate to Twitter and Facebook, not to hear Leninists preach against religion, but to hear ordinary folks discuss parenting, chocolate chip cookie recipes, vaccines, homosexuality issues and even the best lullabies. Thanks to the phenomenon of "social audio" that was launched mid-pandemic, people can satisfy their thirst for office water-cooler chats or free speech from the comfort of their living room or bathtub using platforms like Clubhouse or Twitter Spaces.

This is a lot of control we are giving Big Tech. But offering these companies the benefit of the doubt, I like to think these new platforms are Silicon Valley's way of helping us (and cashing-in) on the pent-up desire for human contact. These new software solutions also arrived just in time as people were exhausted from using more formal virtual video apps like Zoom and Skype.

The early mover was Clubhouse. Launched in April 2020 as an invitation-only audio-chat app, it suddenly become hip in 2021. Twitter has since introduced its own member-only audio chat app, Spaces. In a chat held in March 2021, Twitter CFO Ned Segal said the social media giant would introduce podcast-type recordings clipped from chats conducted on this platform and add a "tip jar" function so hosts can earn money.

Both apps are great examples of how online chats met the demands of the pandemic. With millions working from home or under restrictions, it made plenty of commercial sense to allow a casual, spontaneous chatting experience. It remains to be seen if social audio is just another fad, but it did place a bit more lipstick on Big Tech exactly when a touch-up was badly-needed.

CHAPTER 7

Broken News

The Media as Gardarene Swine

R obert MacNeil's 1998 novel *Breaking News* opens with a vivid keynote speech from a fictional network news anchor Grant Munro. He accuses broadcast media of "behaving like Gardarene swine" in their coverage of a fictional presidential sex scandal.

"You remember, Christ sent evil spirits into a heard of pigs, and the maddened herd raced over a cliff and drowned. I think that in our swollen numbers; in our new and insane competitiveness; in our rising desperation for ratings; our prurient glee in discussing the president's sex life; in our rush to report unsubstantiated rumour, leaks and gossip; an evil spirit entered us, and we became that herd of maddened swine racing towards our own destruction."

Though the obscure reference to deranged pigs was enthusiastically applauded by media colleagues, it hit a trip wire in the minds of media proprietors. Unfortunately for the self-conscious and aging Munro, his speech accelerated a discussion among his managers about whether he had reached his "best by" date.

Today's media herd is not too dissimilar to Munro's caricature. During the Covid-19 pandemic, which overlapped with the pathetic closing chapter of then-US President Donald Trump's tumultuous US presidency, media outlets seemed to abandon long-held standards in a maddening game of one-upmanship. The US cable news networks – FOX, CNN, MSNBC – pivoted from reporting the news to unabashedly spouting opinions almost 24/7. And that raises the question, does the new broadcasting format create the risk of opinion being mistaken by viewers as fact?

As with many other sectors, the pandemic accelerated journalism trends that were already underway such as using cutting-edge technology to enable reporting from home, new funding models that let journalists become solo operators, and American hedge funds swooping in to "save" daily metropolitan newspapers.

As if the Covid-19 lockdowns were not enough, the shift to more opinion news and shorter stories for the public's shrinking attention spans made it harder for journalists to squeeze good reporting into a smaller news hole – especially those reporting from overseas bureaux. Across dozens of media outlets, the once-revered role of foreign correspondent lost its key on-air slot in the daily news schedule, and was pretty much relegated to reporting breaking news. (Speaking of which, most readers would agree that the "breaking news" jingle has now become so abused that it has lost any urgency to rouse us from our lockdown-induced slumbers).

I would pay good money to hear Grant Munro's assessment of the past four years of sensationalist White House coverage. With notable exceptions, I suspect he would find a stronger analogy than unwashed farm animals to describe how American opinion-driven "news" shows acted nearly every day. (To be fair, Trump's blatant lies created a situation where reporting shifted from "who, what, when, where and why" to "he said, they responded" to "you just heard the president lie").

A Splintering Media Ecosystem

Vladimir Lenin reportedly once said: "There are decades where nothing happens; and there are weeks where decades happen." The madness in the wider news industry can partially be explained by the relentless digital disruption. If anything, the pandemic accelerated the changes.

In other words, nails were being driven into the coffin of traditional media well before Covid-19. The disruption caused by social media and internet technology was mostly predictable, and mostly beyond the control of even competent media managers.

For a start, Big Tech giants Facebook and Google now suck up a high percentage of every advertising dollar and leave only crumbs to be divided among the rest of media. The business founded by Mark Zuckerberg as a college dorm experiment in 2003 generated US$84.2 billion from digital advertising in 2020. To get a glimpse of the problem, consider that the venerable *New York Times* only earned a measly US$800 million in digital ad revenue that same year.

Adding to this strangulation are the advanced algorithms built by computer engineers to measure with excruciating accuracy the number of times readers click on a story, how long they linger and if they share the story. Introduced to newsrooms in the mid-2000s, these algorithms have led to the annoying "click bait" headlines crafted precisely to grab one's attention. The data created a feedback loop by lowering the general reader's attention span and convincing media managers to push for even shorter, simpler and tailored copy – called "ornamental" content – for the always-on, mobile generation. The more scandal-packed a story, the better. But this left little time for important stories.

Grant Munro probably wouldn't recognise modern newsrooms anymore. Many have replaced their wall-paper with dozens of flashing LCD screens showing a cage fight of click statistics, time spent on site, top stories, comment counts or best-shared videos. In Munro's day, if your story ended up on the front page of a physical newspaper, "above the fold," you could take a victory lap for writing one of the best stories of the day. Now, the "best story" might only be an inane list of the top-ten friendly dogs, because that's what the algorithm highlighted.

The new tracking systems have angered journalists. At the *Daily Telegraph* in London – which in 2016, was forced by unions to remove devices that monitored whether people were at their desks – journalists are ranked by "stars" measuring article clicks. Somehow this translates to how many subscriptions they drive, and therefore how financially successful each journalist's work has been for the company. "It's grotesque," said one reporter. "Algorithmic commissioning linked to pay is a crime against journalism. It will tip the *Telegraph* down a clickbait plughole." Another system at *Fortune* magazine created to measure byline counts and setting traffic goals sparked so much newsroom anger in March 2021 that reporters went on strike for one day.

(But have the directives from editors really changed? When I was writing about hot, listed tech companies during the dot com bubble, a *Forbes* editor told me that I should focus on stories which "make the stock price move").

During economic downturns, journalists tend to be some of the first to feel the pain of slashed advertising budgets. The same thing happened during Covid-19. Indeed, the carnage in the sector was so widespread that it may be impossible to accurately measure the full damage. All these problems were compounded by the emergence of obscure internet outlets writing about off-kilter views or conspiracy theories. No wonder media owners are losing sleep.

Things may not have been perfect two decades ago, but at least in the days of the fictional Grant Munro the internet was no threat to newspapers. Most people woke up, got dressed and jumped on public transport where we could read a free daily newspaper packed with advertising and stories chosen by an experienced editor, not an algorithm. Fast-forward to today with commuters banished indoors to "work from home" and advertisers already heading for the social media doors, the metro papers have all but vanished.

Consider London's *City AM* newspaper. Published since 2005 with a print run of about 85,000 daily copies, last year it went completely online and temporarily slashed editorial staff salaries by 50%. Another free paper, the *Evening Standard*, was forced to furlough many journalists and also reduced salaries to afford the desperate switch to home delivery just to stay solvent. Finally, the circulation of *Metro*, once Britain's largest newspaper, dropped from about 1.4 million copies to below 500,000 as of April 2020.

Like debt, traditional media's competition with social media had a compounding effect on the quality of news reporting, which led to new budget cuts, which in turn affected quality, and so on back around the cycle.

Jack of All Trades, Master of None

This problem became so acute that most journalists assigned to cover Covid-19 didn't know the first thing about virus stories. After all, the main casualty in the beancounters' relentless cutting of budgets was to generalise or remove all journalists dedicated to a specific topic – the traditional "beat reporter." The modern staff writer has since turned into an efficient jack-of-all-trades, but a master of none. I spent many frustrating days last year watching government officials being given the benefit of the doubt by overwhelmed and underprepared journalists who should have challenged every statement, rather than settle for bland bullet points. But they could not reasonably do otherwise because they simply lacked the deep knowledge of the topic.

The few remaining beat reporters lucky to have a job at some of the larger outlets haven't avoided disruption completely. Many are forced by their editors to be "multimedia journalists" requiring video pieces, social media posts, an online story, updates and much more. Correspondents are also now going live from home using their smartphones to record themselves describing breaking news, lowering standards even further. But, again, there is little else they can do while locked indoors.

The fierce competition with social media for precious advertising dollars is another reason traditional media can no longer afford to hire qualified writers who know their topic. Skill demands payment and the budgets just aren't there. Even the management of the *New Yorker* folded its arms when its journalists pulled a 24-hour strike in January 2021 to protest low salaries. Owner Condé Nast rejected a union offer of a salary floor of US$65,000 which it said would help "remedy decades of underpayment and disparities." Condé Nast countered with a floor of US$45,000 instead. Lindsay Crouse of *The New York Times* commented by saying such a scrawny salary offer was just code for "only apply if your parents pay your rent." In March 2021, after several rounds of fruitless negotiations, *New Yorker* staffers voted for another strike at an undetermined future date.

Former Canadian investigative reporter Victor Malarek said coverage on Covid-19 was "pathetic" since most journalists are now essentially stenographers.

"Newsrooms worldwide have been decimated by owners more interested in advertising revenue than giving journalists the practice time so they can report effectively on big issues. Instead, the flocks of journalist sheep trot from one press conference to another, jotting down the verbiage spewed by politicians and Big Pharma without challenge."

That's a major problem because, whether we like it or not, media outlets are an important part of the public health system since they are responsible for disseminating messages and influencing public behaviour. In a mass casualty event, like a pandemic, health experts must communicate instructions swiftly to the widest possible audience. Most importantly, these messages need to be believable. So, when journalists don't know their topics or elected officials label media as "fake," that can throw the whole communication infrastructure into chaos.

This problem started long before Trump's pompous escalator ride to announce his bid for the White House in June 2016. A Gallup poll that same year found trust in mass media was at a 45-year low, with just 32% of respondents saying they trust media "a great deal" or a "fair amount." Since Trump's election, more people bought into the "fake news" narrative, exacerbating a crisis of confidence in one of the five pillars of democracy, or retreated to comfortable pro-Trump outlets like One America News Network or Fox News.

Meanwhile, Republican officials in the US were habitually ignoring media interview requests, even one from NBC's *Meet the Press* in November 2020 – a Sunday TV broadcast that's been around for pretty much as long as there's been television. After being rebuffed by every Republican politician, host Chuck Todd tweeted: "They all declined." In January 2021, CNN's Daniel Dale asked the rookie Republican congresswoman Marjorie Taylor Greene to comment on a long list of her dubious claims. She responded: "Here's our comment: 'CNN is fake news.'"

The assault on the news media was by not limited to the United States. The government of the world's most populous democracy, India, intimated that holding those in power accountable was no longer part of the press' responsibility, according to the US-based media watchdog Freedom House. One Indian minister reportedly described international journalists critical of New Delhi as "presstitutes."

Journalism on a Ventilator

I witnessed the storm clouds gathering first-hand while in New York City just as the lights were being switched off on Broadway last year.

In-person editorial meetings were already cancelled and my newsroom contacts were all sent home to work remotely. I was one of the last in-studio guests invited to Bloomberg's eerily quiet Manhattan studios to discuss the pandemic. Through the dust from the make-up brushes, I heard managers tell their staff to prepare for indefinite furloughs. That affected me, too. All of a sudden, everyone who relied on staying visible to generate an income quickly downloaded a copy of Zoom or Skype on their home computer. I called peers and tech friends to learn about the best lighting, make-up and tech gadgets so I could create a professional-looking on-air presence, since that seemed to be the new normal for news reporting and for commentators.

As 2020 ended, I heard horror stories from several newsroom executives on both sides of the Atlantic. They told me of staff calling in sick or mentally struggling to juggle work/life pressures at home. By Christmas, a major London-based media outlet sent a few dozen journalists home on a single day due to isolation orders.

But it was hard to imagine a situation worse than in India. By mid-May 2021 a staggering 300 journalists had died due to Covid-19, according to the Network of Women in Media. In one cruel 28-day period, 56 Indian journalists lost their lives – including veteran reporter Rajkumar Keswanil, who warned of the Bhopal gas tragedy in 1984.

According to research from the University of North Carolina, more than a quarter of US outlets, including century-old publications and Pulitzer Prize-winners, vanished in the 15 years leading up to 2020. And since 2018, 300 newspapers have closed and half of all local journalist positions are gone, the study said, as round after round of layoffs left many gutsy dailies and weeklies mere shells of their former Pulitzer Prize-winning selves.

Newsrooms that predicted the online future had the wind at their backs during the crisis, but they were few and far between. Bizarrely, online media giant HuffPost and its owner Verizon Media completely misread the tea leaves when it laid off 7% of staff and eliminated its enterprise health reporting section in 2019. A year later after BuzzFeed acquired HuffPost, it cut 47 US employees and abruptly shuttered its Canadian operations which resulted in the loss of 23 staff.

This was sad, but not surprising. I've seen the changes in the

NPR newsroom in Washington, DC and *The New York Times* headquarters in midtown Manhattan. At both institutions, the space for social media operations was pushing desks dedicated for traditional news coverage to the fringes. At the *Times*, my host said daily front-page news meetings were a thing of the past since online editions are updated in real-time. Due to the (mostly younger) segment of the "always on" population, successful media outlets had already shifted to online-only models to capture the selfie generation. Even the BBC has a special team to create savvy infographics and 30-second video stories with subtitles.

And as everybody's world shrunk during the lockdowns, dozens of friends told me they were sick of reading depressing news and much preferred to follow local events about bike path upgrades or the latest Amazon package theft. "Don't judge me," said one friend in an email. "It's a coping mechanism. I have started checking out our rural community website where I can keep up on lost dogs, cougars getting too close to horses, missing mail or sightings of strangers in the neighbourhood. NOW, THAT'S NEWS!"

Covid-19 may have buried many news outlets but the crisis was a revival period for coverage on school closures or the nearest vaccination and testing location. Obscure news sources like *The Capital Daily* in Victoria, Canada, which specialised in local news, underwent a renaissance.

Unfortunately, some news executives learned about this trend the hard way. When managers at the subsidised Canadian Broadcasting Corporation (CBC) announced at the start of the pandemic a plan to "temporarily" replace local evening newscasts with a national network feed from Toronto, people were outraged. President and chief executive Catherine Tait said at the time many media jobs are difficult to do at home and CBC worried its systems would fail. "The timing couldn't be worse," said a nonprofit set up to protect against CBC cuts. "Shutting down CBC local TV news gives us less of this vital information at precisely the time when we need more of it." In the end, the protests worked and

CBC restored local TV news programmes a week later. But it was a wake-up call for complacent media, nonetheless.

The Technology/Media Bromance

Where information technology was mostly a boon to journalism over the last hundred years, the golem has in a way turned on its master. Two decades into the new century, reporting can now be done from almost anywhere in the world using cheap, mobile and sleek equipment. Expensive satellite links and well-stocked hotel bars have been replaced with compression software and fast broadband internet connections.

All that's been wonderful for journalists, but it also reduced the friction for anyone else to join at the ground floor of news gathering. Smartphones, wifi and social media let normal people quickly provide their own photos or video of breaking news events, ushering in the age of "citizen journalism." The examples of this are too many to count. Ordinary folk in the right place at the right time in 2013 were able to record much of the Boston Marathon bombings and the horrific crash of Asiana Airlines Flight 214 at San Francisco International Airport. And in Iran in January 2020, the regime was forced to admit its culpability in shooting-down a Ukraine International Airliners jet flying over Tehran after a video of the missile strikes was captured by a random pedestrian and uploaded to social media.

And the early days of Covid-19 panic near the outbreak site in China's Hubei province were documented by enterprising citizen journalists, most of whom disappeared or were detained.

Some media stalwarts argue that allowing citizen journalist content to pollute the airwaves unfiltered will deepen the seemingly bottomless fake news swamp. Others suggest the legacy media model is woefully lopsided since it allows news companies to generate revenue by using free or low-cost content and rip off citizen contributors who are in no position to demand proper payment or rights for their work. Clearly, some rebalancing is in order.

To square this circle, the larger media outlets have created a hybrid solution in which citizen journalism is included alongside legacy journalism. CNN's iReport was one of the best examples of such models and at its peak attracted over 100,000 videos, images and text entries in 2012 alone. CNN didn't let just anything play on its feed; all items that made it to air were fully verified by editors and journalists. Segments ranged from an English teacher in the Gaza Strip filming rocket attacks to a retired cop cutting up his National Rifle Association membership card after a school shooting. Although this hybrid model was wildly successful, it was obviously not lucrative. But by the time iReport was retired in 2015 after almost a decade, more than one million people were registered as contributors, which showed that it was popular.

This democratisation of media technology allowed news media to continue broadcasting during lockdowns without skipping a beat since journalists and anchors had the tools to work at home. Viewers became familiar with the house interiors of anchors, journalists, politicians and other guests. Children of interviewees would make unannounced, cameo appearances on livestreams. One particularly delightful example of this was when the daughter of a medical doctor being interviewed popped onto the screen and started questioning the BBC journalist herself (the video was viewed almost two million times on YouTube).

When my friend and CNN anchor Chris Cuomo was struck down by Covid-19 a few months into the pandemic, he carried on with his show from the basement of his house. In one wild episode, he was diagnosed live on air by CNN chief medical correspondent Sanjay Gupta, with Cuomo sweating beads of perspiration and describing in real-time how his household was coping with the illness.

Yet, journalists' reliance on their technology introduced unintended consequences as well. Many news organisations ordered their foreign correspondents to come home but then asked them to continue reporting on events in Beijing or Moscow. During a virtual panel in the fall of 2020, I asked CNN's chief international correspondent Clarissa Ward if she feared reporting from home may deter newsroom managers from sending their correspondents back into the field once the pandemic ended.

"I worry it will. Particularly with organisations that maybe don't have a huge amount of cash. They've seen that it's possible for people to do everything on Zoom from their living room. I fear they'll take the wrong lesson from that and replace on-the-ground reporting permanently.

"I think a lot of foreign correspondents are anxiously thinking: 'where will I get the money to do my next documentary?' Or: 'where am I going to pitch this next story in an atmosphere that increasingly lacks any real excitement or commitment to that kind of story-telling right now,'" Ward said.

Of course, in some locations the usual blocking of journalists doing their job continued regardless of Covid-19 or new technology disruption. Although the pandemic was now being used as an excuse to box out reporters even further.

Natalia Sedletska, founder of an award-winning investigative TV programme for Radio Free Europe/Radio Liberty in Ukraine, told me courts in Ukraine quickly closed hearings to the public on the flimsy pretence of safety but did not provide live-streams of the trials in replacement. Sedletska added that extracting information or tips from sources also got much tougher. After all, in many former Soviet Republics, sources are generally reluctant to speak on the telephone anyway and often prefer to meet in person. This became far more challenging during the lockdowns.

I was lucky – extremely lucky – to time my career in journalism when the skies were the limit, editors had nearly bottomless budgets and well before over-protective security professionals could veto any risky interview. Fat media wallets funded exotic reporting trips that could be the stuff of Hollywood screenplays. I recall travelling to China to write about the aftermath of the Tiananmen Square massacre in 1989. A few weeks later, I was in Myanmar speaking to student protest leaders who survived the urban death squads of that country's previous brutal military coup. Many of these same soldiers are once again killing protesters following another successful coup in February 2021.

In a tale of fatal attraction, my former Hong Kong newspaper dispatched me in 1994 on short notice to the Siberian city of Vladivostok to report on the violent death of a top New Zealand lawyer, apparently lured to Russia by his prostitute girlfriend. I was also tasked by the *South China Morning Post* to my parent's homeland in Ukraine, to report on the breaking up of the Soviet Union and the clean-up efforts at Chornobyl.

And in the mid-1990s, an eccentric Thai editor at *Asia Times* signed-off on a bizarre round-the-world trip from Thailand to Washington, DC so I could meet a former KGB colonel who defected to the US. (My minder was a former CIA agent who somehow ended up on the newspaper's payroll). Later, as a freelancer during the "dot-com bubble," I was assigned several trips to Singapore and Beijing to document the heady days of tech start-ups, which is when I met Katrina Barillova from Chapter Two.

As I look back fondly to those days, I can't help but wonder if today's young journalists, who dream of overseas assignments, will ever convince their editors to once again send them beyond the city limits. As CNN's Clarissa Ward said, even if these postings can be expensive, they will remain important. Especially in the post-Covid era.

Some Hope

I believe the rumours of the death of journalism are mostly exaggerated. Whatever world emerges in the so-called "new normal" after the pandemic will still need professional reporters to keep dictators honest, hold corporations to high standards and prevent police from tarnishing their badge's reputation. In fact, several journalists distinguished themselves during the pandemic, among them SKY News' Cordelia Lynch, the BBC's Yogita Limaye, Fergus Walsh and Clive Myrie, and Pulitzer Prize-winning US science journalist Laurie Garrett. Also from the BBC, Stephen

McDonnell provided heroic reporting from Beijing and Wuhan.

Cashflow will remain a problem but new business models are already maturing to keep quality journalists on the beat. And it must be acknowledged that revenue from the relatively new digital side of news operations is helping to subsidise traditional journalism and investigative reporting.

I also believe that with proper vetting and decent remuneration, citizen journalists will be encouraged to stay in the mix, too. This hybrid media model can lean on support from crowdfunding and the billions of dollars available from foundations and wealth funds rather than compete directly with social media for a withering advertising dollar. Done right, it can all help pay for high-quality journalism well into the future.

The Spain-based online newspaper *El Español* is already forging the way ahead. For its launch in 2015, it raised US$3.98 million in just two months from 5624 patrons. The scrappy media startup allows readers a certain number of free articles before presenting them with a paywall. Amid the punishing lockdowns, the paper recorded about 20 million monthly unique readers and rivals the readership of much larger outlets like *El Pais* and *El Mundo*. Across the Atlantic in the US, multi-platform media startup The Young Turks raised US$2 million in 2017 to hire extra investigative teams. It calls itself "America's largest online progressive show" and its impressive 200 million monthly views may actually justify that description.

Crowdfunding and subscription platforms have mostly survived Covid-19, but they may only be part of the long-term solution for saving media. After all, many potential donors, subscribers and pay-per-view readers will be struggling to keep a roof over their heads for the foreseeable future. But crowd-funded publications do suffer far less pressure from government, big business and advertisers, so they can go the extra mile in investigations. "We certainly believe the more you depend on subscribers, the easier it is to be independent," said *El Español* co-founder María Ramírez.

But the birth of a new media model won't be easy. The Dutch/English-language start-up *The Correspondent*, which raised US$2.6 million for its launch in 2018 and kept itself alive with subscriptions, had to shut its doors in January 2021. Its problem wasn't funding, it was that people wanted better access to local news and since the outlet wasn't providing it, subscribers went somewhere else. Founders Rob Wijnberg and Ernst-Jan Pfauth wrote in a farewell letter to readers that they made a mistake in succumbing to the pressure of covering the Covid-19 pandemic which left little energy for "un-breaking news."

Xanthe Scharff, co-founder of the independent newsroom *The Fuller Project*, a nonprofit dedicated to ground-breaking journalism about women, told me many high-net-worth individuals see the demise of local news as damaging to democracy. Non-profits like hers are stepping into this "mushrooming" media niche which is already increasing local news coverage and fostering "a real public service mentality," Scharff said.

From Mass Media to Silo Journalism

Silicon Valley has given us game-changing disruption from food delivery, book publishing and perhaps even getting to the surface of Mars. But are these billionaire geeks now aiming their laser pens towards the pock-marked media landscape as well?

That may be happening right now as you read this book.

Media outlets, both big and small, became the beneficiaries of Silicon Valley largesse last year. It started when Amazon founder Jeff Bezos bought the *Washington Post* for US$250 million in 2013 after agreeing to a pitch by the paper's founding family to use his "mastery of the Internet" to restore some sparkle on the crown jewel among media royalty.

Already, big names like venture capital firm Andreessen Horowitz (known for investments in Facebook, Airbnb and Slack), which has a cool US$16.5 billion in assets under management, upgraded its own blog post feed and podcast with a goal to "make sense of technology, innovation and where things are going." The fund hired former *Wall Street Journal* and CNN reporter Maggie Leung to help sell the idea as a serious media initiative.

Substack, another Horowitz-backed paywall email newsletter, already has about 500,000 subscribers as of April 2021. Co-founder Hamish McKenzie, in brash prose that could only come from Silicon Valley, said the reason people were so attracted to the service was because it had "no addiction-maximising feeds, autoplaying videos or retweetable quotes to suck you into a psychological space you never asked to be in. You make decisions about which information to put into your brain based on how well certain writers reward your trust, not based on a dopamine hit gained by refreshing a feed packed with performative posturing," he said.

Whether it works or not and these new platforms deliver us salvation from 'the attention economy', expect more money to be thrown around by tech denizens hoping to build their own media empires. In 2018, venture capitalist Peter Thiel (not exactly a friend of the media) was rumoured to sink huge funding into a new cable news network to rival FOX News. And in May 2021, New York-based hedge fund Alden Global Capital, known for eviscerating newspapers it acquired, spent US$630 million to buy a legendary chain of US dailies including the *Baltimore Sun*, *Chicago Tribune* and the *New York Daily News*.

Facebook, which has drawn much ire from media companies for letting their news content be shared for free, perhaps felt some guilt at the part it played in helping to gut newsrooms. In an act of contrition, the Big Tech giant, months into the pandemic, announced it was setting aside US$100 million to support local news in the US and globally. Zuckerberg let it slip in January 2021 that his team is developing a newsletter tool for freelancers and independent writers as well. Not to be outdone, Twitter dipped its feet into "long form journalism" at around the same time, with the purchase of Revue, a five-year-old Dutch newsletter platform.

Where is this all going? My gut feeling says that unlike the disruption of automation in other areas, journalism will always depend on human talent to get the job done. This pandemic was an accelerant for trends that were already underway, such as algorithms reporting on the weather, for instance. I forecast a mixed business model for media as outlets and writers survive on funding from governments, foundations, wealth funds, crowd sourcing and, to a lesser extent, advertising or paid subscriptions. But do not discount the role of obscure sources of funding like the one which bankrolled my former newspaper, *Asia Times*. That outlet ceased its print publication in 1997 just as its eccentric publisher, Sondhi Limthongkul, declared bankruptcy and swapped his Versace suits for saffron Buddhist robes. (*Asia Times* still survives to this day as an online publication).

And, when I refer to obscure sources of funding, I include Russia and China. The latter is well down the road already in terms of influencing narratives in Hollywood. Mass media, social media and film will increasingly become part of their arsenal to create disruption and confusion in the West and more broadly.

With all this change happening in such an important sector, strap in for what is bound to be an interesting ride!

Epilogue

So, what about the future? How will life change after the Covid-19 pandemic? Before I can answer those questions, the pandemic must end. At the time of writing, vaccines are slowly rolling out but fresh viral strains are still emerging in multiple countries. On top of that, new and restarted military conflicts – including in the Middle East – along with diplomatic spats will make widespread vaccination a much more difficult process than it needs to be.

Nevertheless, below is a tentative list of predictions. The net is cast broadly, but these points may come in handy for anyone planning to navigate this new normal:

1. As pro-democracy movements and authoritarian leaders face off, expect those in power to strike back hard by using the tools they know best – forcing internet companies into compliance, adding new regulations, throttling social media platforms, or even shutting down communications;

2. Touchless commercial transactions will become the norm and physical cash will go extinct. China will be among the first to transition to a complete digitisation of its currency. Such digital currencies will also be used to track people's spending and consumption through a "social credit score" digital system;

3. Tele-health will undergo a massive adoption spurt, especially in large countries where millions remain deprived of a decent standard of healthcare. This in turn will make healthcare accessible and reduce both the time and resources needed to apply it. Hospital visits will be less necessary;

4. Tens of millions will switch on the internet for the first time. In the developed world, much of this new adoption will be fuelled by a series of coordinated "Build Back Better" stimulus projects. In the developing world, wealthy foundations and Big Tech will help connect the digitally underserved by using satellites and, if costs drop, even by launching self-navigating "internet balloons" the size of a tennis court;

5. The traumatic memory of lockdowns could encourage kids to go outside again and spend less time glued to their screens. Conversely, their fear of the outdoors might grow and result in children spending even more time with screens;

6. Travel will change forever. Those who can afford a break will take more sensible and fewer overseas trips. Expect higher demand for motorhomes, camping and chartered jet travel to remote locations with private accommodations. Business travel will resume but at nowhere near the level of 2019. The cruise ship industry will be the last sector to recover. "Vaccine passports" will be required to cross borders;

7. University campuses may never be the same. Distance learning will pressure college administrators to rethink their entire business model. Interest in the trades will increase as high school graduates consider how to "recession-proof" their careers. To encourage diversity and fill crucial skills gaps, firms will loosen university degree requirements and begin to offer more apprenticeships;

8. Printed media will continue to disappear and change how journalism is performed. In newsrooms, beancounters will raise the bar for funding on everything from foreign postings to investigative journalism. Expect interest in local news to stay high. Remote reporting and freelancers will be more in demand. Silicon Valley and Wall Street largesse will increasingly step in to support all kinds of

journalism – but frequently in exchange for brutal profit maximisation and efficiency benchmarks;

9. Artificial intelligence, Big Data and the internet of things (boosted by 5G networks) will help prevent future pandemics and hasten the development of life saving vaccines;

10. The robustness of supply chains will be re-evaluated under a "never again" mindset. China's status as the supplier and warehouse of the world's medical supplies will be challenged;

11. Big Tech – especially social media – will face greater regulations and anti-trust legislation for allowing disinformation to spread uncontrolled. In authoritarian countries, tech companies will be forced to accept draconian censorship rules to retain market share. Personal data will become self-sovereign, meaning individuals can earn money from businesses wishing to profit from it;

12. More female leaders will be voted into office, as voters emerge from the pandemic with the view that women tend to make better family and community-friendly decisions;

13. Social media "influencers" won't be as influential. Partly because travel will remain restricted and due to brands asking influencers to prove a demonstrable return on investment. Brands will place more of a premium on securing Gen Z influencers with paid partnerships;

14. Brands doing business in China will be pressured to back away from social activism, keep silent on human rights abuses and avoid criticism of the Chinese government, even if it risks giving up significant market share in the West;

15. Even so, suspicion of China will grow even as the country turns more inwards, and it will no longer be a welcoming place for foreign companies. Companies doing business in China will be expected to share their technology;

16. In-person dating will return and Zoom fatigue will set in;

17. New work collaboration tools will make working from home easier, which will change inner cities and lower the need for public infrastructure. Expect hybrid models of work as people continue to crave human contact;
18. Foreign service postings for diplomacy will be scarcer as more work transitions to remote or online. However, fewer boots on the ground will also mean conflicts last longer or be deprived of early resolution;
19. Smart medical clothing and wearables will become commonplace. The private sector will also demand new devices to monitor illness (i.e., temperature). Visits to a friends' house may involve some sort of health screening;
20. Many governments will retain much of the enhanced emergency powers granted during the pandemic to keep better tabs on their citizens – and on political opponents;
21. Patterns of consumption will change, particularly with more online shopping. This may include the rise in a "buy local" attitude. People will also dine in more frequently rather than visit restaurants;
22. The work from home trend will impact participation in everything from sports and charities to community organisations. People of faith will participate in more virtual worship services;
23. Trust in elected leaders, public health officials and experts will decline as citizens deal with the economic implications of draconian public health orders. In jurisdictions that handled the pandemic exceptionally well, leaders will enjoy a surge in support;
24. Social audio – i.e., Clubhouse and Twitter Spaces – may prove to be a fad as device fatigue worsens and people go back to the outdoors;
25. Medical science collaboration will increase as experts learn to work across time zones. However, cross-border collaboration will segregate among blocs of nations;
26. Vaccines will be used for political or public relations

purposes. Authoritarian countries manufacturing the vaccines will "donate" to curry favour with smaller countries. More countries will become self-reliant in vaccine development;

27. To further spread confusion, Russia and China will devote more resources to influencing the Western media narratives along with bankrolling their own outlets and social media war rooms. Western superpowers will counter with their own tactics, aided by technology.

28. In the sectors of travel, health, finance, real estate and beyond, the middleman will face an existential threat from the use of more technology.

Some of these may sound frightening, but I retain a good measure of optimism about the near future. But as this book robustly shows, it will be important for any technological breakthrough and vaccine development to be shared evenly so no one is left behind.

In the meantime, defeating the virus will depend not on vaccines or technology – but on human behaviour. For a start, world leaders must dig deep to summon the political will to impose unpopular epidemic containment measures. Although the data and what we know about Covid-19 will continue to change, the appearance of flip-flopping hurts public trust in those institutions. Health officials can offset this risk by learning better public communication skills.

Many of the elderly victims of Covid-19 had survived terrible events when they were younger only to be struck down by an invisible virus in such an undignified, abrupt and vicious manner. This should be a reminder for everyone that no one is invincible and that it is too easy to take for granted simple things like visiting grandparents or regularly washing our hands. Covid-19 proved normal life can change in an instant, so it is important to make the most of every day.

This book is a clarion call to leverage the "good" side of

technology and to reach out to others living with loneliness, hopelessness or depression. These invisible symptoms are particularly insidious, just like a virus. The battle against Covid-19 may eventually be won, but the mental trauma and distress from this episode is just beginning to be felt. Used cleverly and in moderation, technology can guide us through the looming recovery phase and we may begin to see devices as our friend, rather than an invasion into our lives. Perhaps the legacy of the Covid-19 pandemic will be to change technology from "bad" to "good"? Only time will tell.

Acknowledgements

M y late professor and father, Bohdan Bociurkiw, frequently reminded his mentees to "publish or perish" to avoid involuntary banishment to academia purgatory.

While I'm not an academic, the memory of his stubborn perseverance to finish a book on church-state politics in the former Soviet Union helped me reach the finish line for *Digital Pandemic*.

I am truly blessed to have such constant support and encouragement of family, friends, colleagues and members of my network. The list is long.

To my friends and mentors, Michael Popow and Natalie Billon. Time and again, they seem to have a knack for sensing when I needed a boost of chutzpah. They've kept me on track, especially in the depths of lockdown, encouraging me to make sense of what's going on, connect the dots and be first off the starting block with a new discovery.

Victor Malarek, who boosted me up the journalism ladder in my early career and stayed with me through the decades as a dear friend, mentor and sounding board on everything from job-hops to book ideas. Victor's bullshit meter and nose for scandal are second to none!

Captain David Campbell for his never-failing inquiries into the book progress, for his support of this book and for teaching me the finer points of maritime navigation and etiquette.

My dear friends on the other side of the British Columbia-Washington state line who, through a 2020 birthday celebration and countless Thursday evening virtual Happy Hours, kept a smile on my face and loneliness at bay during lockdowns. Their collective support and encouragement, including for the book launch, meant more than words can express. Jennifer Jedda kindly volunteered as a daily point of contact during an especially challenging 14-day stretch of writing in self-quarantine and supplied excellent feedback on my earlier manuscript.

My colleagues at CNN Opinion, who over years of collaboration on op-ed pieces, truly helped improved my critical writing skills by challenging my assumptions and pushing me to strengthen my arguments.

Dr. Sue Varma for convincing me to write myself into the book as much as possible, and for her insightful quotes, feedback and valuable introductions to sources.

For her encouragement, savvy ideas and boundless energy – the wonderful Farzana Baduel of Curzon PR in London.

To my peer mentor, Lina Duque, for her exceptional peer mentoring and friendship.

Georgios Pokas for encouraging me to soar as high as I possibly can. My Global Impact podcast co-host, Melissa Ricci, for her helpful advice and efforts to promote this book.

Friends overseas (you know who you are) who agreed to vet certain chapters for errors and for any red flags which could haunt me later. Special thanks to Sofiya for her encouragement, savvy research skills and sharp eye for spotting gaps.

My brother, Taras, for donating long hours of proofreading and for sharing his knowledge of self-publishing. Roger Barliszen for his feedback and brotherly cajoling to get the job done.

The Ukrainian Credit Union for their support of the precursor to this book, *Digital Crack*.

Gudrun for accepting me as a writer-in-residence in Portugal, along with Debbie and Hedley for making that sabbatical happen. Yurij for unparalleled hospitality and Uliana for always asking "when will the book be finished?"

In California, Deisy Suarez-Giles for her never-ending support, encouraging talks, and affection; Keith Giles for his expertise and companionship; and Jasmine Boussem for reading some content and compelling me to publish.

Nathan Smith of FirstEdit Services in faraway New Zealand, for finding me, and for his professional editing of this book. I highly recommend him unreservedly to others.

Also in New Zealand, Antonina Elliott of QuriousWorld Ltd., for her wonderful book graphics and pleasant brainstorming sessions. And in London, my editorial assistant, Preeti Bali, for her valuable fact-checking skills, encouragement and logistics prowess.

The supportive staff at the London Speaker Bureau and Specialist Speakers for their representation.

To anyone else I've unintentionally missed – a huge thank you.

And finally, to you – the reader – for purchasing this book and recommending it to others.

Notes

Dedication Page

1. **Dr. Li Wenliang**: Li is credited with being the first medical professional to sound the alarm on the outbreak of Covid-19 in Wuhan weeks before he contracted the illness himself and died. See: *China's Hero Doctor was Punished for Telling Truth About Coronavirus*, by Michael Bociurkiw, CNN Opinion, February 11, 2020, https://www.cnn.com/2020/02/08/opinions/coronavirus-bociurkiw/index.html

2. **Zhang Zhan, Fang Bin, Chen Qiushi and Li Zehua**: These four were citizen journalists in China who provided extensive coverage on social media during the first weeks of the Covid-19 outbreak in China. Li, Fang and Chen have all disappeared. Li Zehua re-appeared after almost two months. In March 2021, Chen was reportedly back with his parents and under surveillance. See: *Wuhan Citizen Journalist Chen Qiushi Under Surveillance but may Escape Prosecution*, South China Morning Post, March 31, 2021, https://www.scmp.com/news/china/politics/article/3127786/wuhan-citizen-journalist-chen-qiushi-under-surveillance-may. Zhang, a former lawyer from Shanghai, was sentenced to four years in prison. See: *They Documented the Coronavirus Crisis in Wuhan. Then They Vanished*, The New York Times, February 14, 2020, https://www.nytimes.com/2020/02/14/business/wuhan-coronavirus-journalists.html

Forward

1. **"a forest fire looking for human wood to burn:"** interview with Dr. Michael Osterholm for Global Impact podcast, December 8, 2020, https://anchor.fm/michael-bociurkiw/episodes/S2-E10-In-Conversation-With-Infectious-Disease-Expert-Dr--Michael-Osterholm-envpfn/a-a45nl0l

2. **like California governor Gavin Newsom:** *Photos Raise Doubts About Newsom's Claim That Dinner With Lobbyist was Outdoors Amid Covid-19 Surge*, Los Angeles Times, November 18, 2020, https://www.latimes.com/california/story/2020-11-18/newsom-french-laundry-dinner-explanation-photos-jason-kinney-california-medical-association-covid-19

3. **a report released in mid-March 2021:** *Many Americans Continue to Experience Mental Health Difficulties as Pandemic Enters Second Year,* Pew Research Center, March 16, 2021, https://www.pewresearch.org/fact-tank/2021/03/16/many-americans-continue-to-experience-mental-health-difficulties-as-pandemic-enters-second-year/

4. **"Covid-19 brought all of our divides:"** *America Shows Troubling Warning Signs of a Slide Into Civil War,* Janine di Giovanni, Medium, October 26, 2020, https://gen.medium.com/i-cover-civil-wars-the-state-of-america-right-now-makes-me-anxious-59320249de03

5. **"if the Covid-19 pandemic response":** *A Glimmer of Light for World Action Against the Next Pandemic,* Michael Bociurkiw, CNN Opinion, March 31, 2021, https://www.cnn.com/2021/03/31/opinions/who-pandemic-treaty-opinion-bociurkiw/index.html

Chapter 1: The Big Read

1. **in 2003 the region looked on helplessly:** *Severe Acute Respiratory Syndrome (SARS),* Centers for Disease Control and Prevention, May 3, 2005, https://www.cdc.gov/sars/about/faq.html

2. **scientists eventually dubbed:** *Naming the Coronavirus Disease (Covid-19) and the Virus That Causes It,* World Health Organization, February 11, 2020, https://www.who.int/emergencies/diseases/novel-coronavirus-2019/technical-guidance/naming-the-coronavirus-disease-(covid-2019)-and-the-virus-that-causes-it

3. **marks the first time in modern history:** Sony Kapoor, The Debate: Stuck at Home: How to satisfy Humanity's Urge to Roam?, France 24, December 23, 2020, https://www.france24.com/en/tv-shows/

the-debate/20201223-stuck-at-home-how-to-satisfy-humanity-s-urge-to-roam

4. **"every single human being"**: Ibid.

5. **consider that about 346 million:** *Lack of Access to the Internet is a Barrier for Students and Families Around the World, Especially During the Covid-19 Pandemic,* Meghana Srivatsa, UNICEF, April 3, 2020, https://www.unicefusa.org/stories/digi-tal-disparity-why-universal-internet-access-matters/37159#:~:-text=About%2029%20percent%20of%20youth,6%2C000%20languages%20in%20use%20today

6. **in Africa alone:** *Working Together to Create Africa 2.0,* World Bank, April 9, 2019, https://blogs.worldbank.org/youth-transforming-africa/working-together-create-africa-20

7. **according to a joint report:** *e-Conomy SEA 2020. Resilient and Racing Ahead: Southeast Asia at Full Velocity,* November 10, 2020, Google, Temasek and Bain & Company, https://www.bain.com/insights/e-conomy-sea-2020/

8. **"medical grade Covid-19 screening at scale":** BiointelliSense ad, 2021, https://biointellisense.com/biobutton

9. **"living through a pandemic":** Margit Wennmachers, *Doubling Down on the Future,* a16z.com, January 21, 2021, https://a16z.com/2021/01/25/doubling-down-marketing-update-new-media/

10. **I sat down with Bloomberg Television:** Interview on Balance of Power with David Westin, March 13, 2020, https://youtu.be/Xzzv6263sr8

11. **"we have to do things in our homes":** interview with Abigail Posner, March 8, 2020.

12. **a South Korean man was wrongly accused:** A South Korean law passed in response to the Middle East respiratory syndrome (MERS) in 2015 allows authorities to use personal financial information, cell tower data and CCTV footage in contact tracing. After too much detail was published online by regional govern-ments, the South Korean Centers for Disease Control Prevention released new guidelines in March 2020 limiting the scope and the period of the data disclosure and recommended the deletion of outdated information (after 14 days from the last contact). See:

Why Many Countries Failed at Covid Contact-Tracing — But Some Got it Right, Nature, December 14, 2020, https://www.nature.com/articles/d41586-020-03518-4

13. **on the extreme end:** *Jeffrey Toobin Fired From The New Yorker After Exposing Himself on a Zoom Call*, CNN, November 11, 2020, https://www.cnn.com/2020/11/11/media/jeffrey-toobin-fired-new-yorker/index.html

14. **Canadian member of parliament:** *Liberal MP Apologizes After Appearing Naked on House of Commons Video Feed*, CBC News, April 14, 2021, https://www.cbc.ca/news/politics/william-amos-liberal-mp-naked-parliament-1.5988128

15. **when international student exchanges:** *French learners can sign up for video chats with lonely elderly people in France*, December 7, 2020, https://www.thelocal.fr/20201207/share-ami-french-learners-can-sign-up-for-video-chats-with-lonely-elderly-in-france-for-language-training/

16. **"I believe Covid-19":** *Rock Jones, As Pandemic Wears On, Colleges and Universities Grapple With How to Survive*, PBS The Newshour, January 25, 2021, https://www.pbs.org/newshour/show/pandemics-toll-on-higher-education-leaves-some-institutions-fighting-for-survival

17. **tried to level the technological playing field in its favour:** While most economies registered zero growth in 2020, China's economy expanded by 2.3% and set a target for 6% in 2021, even though it was responsible for the virus. See: *China Rebounds With Economic Growth Target Above 6%*, BBC News, March 5, 2021, https://www.bbc.com/news/business-56289063

18. **"[the pandemic] has inhibited":** Peter Mauer in conversation with me on *Global Impact*, October 24, 2020, https://anchor.fm/michael-bociurkiw/episodes/S2-E5-In-Conversation-with-Peter-Maurer--ICRC-ekfnta

19. **"without the normal constraints":** interview with Abigail Posner, March 8, 2020.

20. **the Committee to Protect Journalists:** Committee to Protect Journalists, *Record Number of Journalists Jailed Worldwide*, December 15, 2020, https://cpj.org/reports/2020/12/record-number-journalists-jailed-imprisoned/

21. **"we danced, rode bikes, swam near whales":** Tweet by Kim Kardashian West, October 27, 2020, https://twitter.com/ KimKardashian/status/1321151224889151490?s=20

22. **an over-confident cruise ship company:** *SeaDream Cancels Remaining 2020 Cruises Following Covid Outbreak*, CNN, November 17, 2020, https://www.cnn.com/travel/article/caribbean-cruises-canceled-seadream-covid/index.html

23. **the scenario brought back horrific memories:** *27 Days in Tokyo Bay: What Happened on the Diamond Princess*, Wired, April 30, 2020, https://www.wired.com/story/ diamond-princess-coronavirus-covid-19-tokyo-bay/

24. **in May 2020 it was reported:** *JetBlue's Founder Helped Fund a Stanford Study That Said the Coronavirus Wasn't That Deadly*, BuzzFeed News, May 15, 2020, https:// www.buzzfeednews.com/article/stephaniemlee/ stanford-coronavirus-neeleman-ioannidis-whistleblower

25. **"a great accelerator of the acceptance":** Conversation with Christine Harada, April, 2021.

26. **"those words ring a little bit hollow":** *What's Driving a Covid-19 Surge in California*, PBS The Newshour, December 25, 2020, https://www.pbs.org/newshour/show/ whats-driving-a-covid-19-surge-in-california

27. **those who did survive:** *Coronavirus: 31 Dead, Elderly Covered in Feces at Dorval Long-term Care Facility*, Global News, April 11, 2020, https://globalnews.ca/news/6807585/ coronavirus-dorval-residence/

28. **Dr. Ryan accused hospitals:** *WHO's Mike Ryan: We're Paying the Price for Running Health Services 'Like Low-Coast Airlines,'* Thomson Reuters, November 30, 2020, https://www.breakingnews.ie/world/whos-mike-ryan-were-paying-the-price-for-running-health-services-like-low-cost-airlines-1044408.html

29. **"this virus has unmasked the importance":** interview on CBC News, April 16, 2021, https://www.instagram.com/tv/ CNyQKHZFnFj/?igshid=m46z3c7id94z

30. **by summer of 2020 the corpse that was once:** blog post, Michael Bociurkiw, May 6, 2020, https://www.michaelbociurkiw.com/ news/2020/5/6/coronavirus-pandemic-latest-update-may-6-2020

31. **Dr. Anastasiya Vasilyeva:** Conversation on Global Impact podcast, May 10, 2020, https://anchor.fm/michael-bociurkiw/episodes/Episode-10-In-Conversation-with-Dr--Anastasia-Vasilyeva-edshek

32. **Dr. Boris Lushniak:** Conversation on Global Impact podcast, May 2, 2020, https://anchor.fm/michael-bociurkiw/episodes/Episode-9-In-Conversation-with-Dr--Boris-Lushniak-edhng6

33. **one pilot in Malaysia:** *'Don't Know if I'll Ever Fly Again:' Pilots, Aircrew in Malaysia Turn Entrepreneurs to Tide Over Covid-19*, February 5, 2021, Channel News Asia, https://www.channelnewsasia.com/news/asia/malaysia-covid-19-pilots-flight-attendants-terminated-retrenched-13698010

34. **the Boeing 747 'Queen of the skies' landed in the scrap heap:** The first Boeing 747 took to the skies in February 1969. According to Cirium, about 500 are still flying, of which 30 are actively carrying passengers, 300 carry cargo (cargo operations remained buoyant during the pandemic) and the remainder are in storage. Along with the once-invincible 747, the gas guzzling double decker Airbus A380 was poised to be phased out by many airlines. See: *British Airways Retires Entire 747 Fleet After Travel Downturn*, BBC, July 17, 2020, https://www.bbc.com/news/business-53426886

35. **one example was proline**: *In Ottawa's Rush to Buy PPE, Companies With Little or no Experience Got Some of the Biggest Contracts*, December 13, 2020, CBC News, https://www.cbc.ca/news/business/ppe-covid-coronavirus-personal-protective-equipment-politics-1.5831340

36. **"for the right kind of hustler"**: *Why Didn't I Make Millions Selling PPE During the Pandemic*, Henry Mance, Financial Times, November 20, 2020, https://www.ft.com/content/b72caa83-e5e1-44a2-b3ff-8c5c09525a06

37. **the collective wealth of the richest 651 Americans:** *US Billionaire Wealth Surges Past $1 Trillion Since Beginning of Pandemic - Total Grows to $4 Trillion*, Institute for Policy Studies, December 9, 2020, https://ips-dc.org/global-billionaire-wealth-surges-4-trillion-over-pandemic/

38. **speaking of Amazon:** Ibid.

39. **but that was nothing compared:** Ibid.

40. **explained why large companies performed so well:** Tweet, May 20, 2020, https://twitter.com/Gary_D_Cohn/ status/1263195806032695297?s=20

41. **yet not every big firm was prepared:** Tesco Record Christmas; Primark Warns of £1bn Sales Loss, Daily Business Group, January 14, 2021, https://dailybusinessgroup.co.uk/2021/01/ tesco-record-christmas-primark-warns-of-1bn-loss-of-sales/

42. **however, this profit jump:** Ibid.

43. **France's finance minister:** *France Welcomes US Pivot on Big Tech Taxes, Sees Potential for a Deal This Spring,* CNBC, January 25, 2021, https://www.cnbc.com/2021/01/25/tax-france-welcomes-us-pivot-on-big-tech-sees-potential-for-a-deal-this-spring.html

44. **as far back as March:** Interview with CNN Newsroom, March 15, 2020, https://www.youtube.com/watch?v=ZGABPOB9DxY

45. **in the US:** *Nearly 74 Million Essential Workers at high Risk for Covid in US,* US News & World Report, November 9, 2020, https://www.usnews.com/news/health-news/articles/2020-11-09/ nearly-74-million-essential-workers-at-high-risk-for-covid-in-us

46. **found that 76% of low-income workers:** *How the Coronavirus Outbreak Has – and Hasn't – Changed the Way Americans Work,* Pew Research Center, December 9, 2020, https://www.pewresearch.org/social-trends/2020/12/09/how-the-coronavirus-outbreak-has-and-hasnt-changed-the-way-americans-work/

47. **in the US alone:** *How Women are Disproportionately Carrying the Cost of Covid,* PBS The NewsHour, December 10, 2020, https://www.pbs.org/wnet/chasing-the-dream/stories/ women-disproportionately-carrying-cost-of-covid/

48. **by the end of 2020:** *2.5 Million Women Left the Work Force During the Pandemic. Harris Sees a 'National Emergency,'* The New York Times, February 18, 2021, https://www.nytimes.com/2021/02/18/ us/politics/women-pandemic-harris.html

49. **in late 2020:** *The CEO of Europe's Biggest Fashion Site is Stepping Down so he Can Prioritize His Wife's Career,* Business Insider, December 7, 2020, https://www.businessinsider.com/zalando-ceo-rubin-ritter-steps-down-prioritize-wife-career-2020-12

50. **"kids have to get their school work":** Conversation on the Global Impact podcast, June 16, 2020, https://anchor.fm/michael-boci-urkiw/episodes/Episode-15-Smartphones--Fintech-Amid-the-Covid-19-Pandemic-eff9lb

51. **a Bain & Company report said:** *e-Conomy SEA 2020. Resilient and Racing Ahead: Southeast Asia at Full Velocity*, November 10, 2020, Google, Temasek and Bain & Company, https://www.bain.com/insights/e-conomy-sea-2020/

52. **"I was offering sunset and moonlight massage":** interview, April 8, 2021.

53. **with the increased awareness:** interview with Christine Harada in April, 2021.

54. **an adventure is a crisis:** in conversation with me on the Sustainability in Action virtual panel by Peak Partners, December 15, 2020. https://www.youtube.com/watch?v=zBToTCWSE5c

Chapter 2: Wearable Tech - From Catwalk to Inside Your Head

1. **at the annual Consumer Electronics Show:** CES award announcement, January 2021, https://ces.tech/Innovation-Awards/Honorees/2021/Honorees/E/Ettie.aspx

2. **US-based smart tool company:** Plott's Ettie claims to be the first infrared temperature sensing video doorbell with 2-way voice communication, https://www.letsplott.com/ettie

3. **and for the ultimate geek,** *This Smart Face Mask Pairs With Your Phone and has Built-in Earbuds,* Input, September 24, 2020, https://www.inputmag.com/style/maskfone-smart-face-mask-built-in-wireless-earbuds

4. **other masks have built-in sensors:** *Masks, Air Purifiers and Other Gadgets Trying to Protect us From Covid-19 Unveiled at CES 2021,* USA Today, January 12, 2021, https://www.usatoday.com/story/tech/2021/01/12/mask-air-purifier-covid-pandemic-gear-unveiled-ces-2021/6635983002/

5. **products like this pushed:** *Shipments of Wearable Devices Leap to 125 Million Units, Up 35.1% in the Third Quarter, According*

to IDC, International Data Corporation, December 2, 2020, https://www.idc.com/getdoc.jsp?containerId=prUS47067820

6. **apple watch:** Ibid.

7. **further, Forrester research:** *How Enterprise Smart Glasses Will Drive Workforce Enablement,* Forrester Research, April 21, 2016, https://www.forrester.com/report/How+Enterprise+Smart+Glasses+Will+Drive+Workforce+Enablement/-/E-RES133722#

8. **one of the earliest players:** source: https://www.spectacles.com/ca-en/shop/spectacles-3/#overview

9. **photos and videos:** Ibid.

10. **"privacy advocates have voiced alarm":** Automated Facial Recognition in the Public and Private Sectors: Report Prepared by the Research Group of the Office of the Privacy Commissioner of Canada, March 2013, https://www.priv.gc.ca/en/opc-actions-and-decisions/research/explore-privacy-research/2013/fr_201303/

11. **Singaporean officials apparently didn't get the memo:** TraceTogether Privacy Safeguards, Singapore Government TraceTogether website, January 2021, https://www.tracetogether.gov.sg/common/privacystatement/

12. **screens are now in front of our eyes:** *Tony Fadell Talks Screen Addiction,* Surface Magazine, 2018, https://vimeo.com/259193418

13. **the average adult American:** *These Updated Stats About How Often You Use Your Phone Will Humble You,* Inc, November 19, 2019, https://www.inc.com/john-brandon/these-updated-stats-about-how-often-we-use-our-phones-will-humble-you.html

14. **and spending:** *Americans Devout More Than 10 Hours-a-day to Screen Time, and Growing,* Bart Pursel, Penn State University, February 21, 2018, https://sites.psu.edu/ist110pursel/2018/02/21/americans-devout-more-than-10-hours-a-day-to-screen-time-and-growing/

15. **psychologist Larry Rosen:** interview, April 2018.

16. **wearable device developed by design student:** Tweet by Reuters, December 22, 2020, https://twitter.com/Reuters/status/1341454709064949763?s=20

17. **younger people more easily adapt:** Conversation with Heidi Lehmann on the Global Impact podcast, December 12, 2020, https://anchor.fm/michael-bociurkiw/episodes/S2-E9-Wearable-Technology--Jimmy-Lai-Sentencing-in-HK--US-elections--Covid-19-enku9q

18. **in October 2020:** *Future of Jobs Report,* World Economic Forum, October, 2020, http://www3.weforum.org/docs/WEF_Future_of_Jobs_2020.pdf

19. **"we've seen the gap increase":** *An Olympian, a Therapist, Professionals: A Look at the Rioters Stocked by Extremism,* PBS NewsHour Weekend, January 16, 2021, https://www.pbs.org/newshour/show/an-olympian-a-therapist-professionals-a-look-at-the-rioters-stoked-by-extremism

20. **"I suspect because of how long":** interview with Dr. Larry Rosen on Global Impact, April 16, 2021, https://anchor.fm/michael-bociurkiw/episodes/S3-E7-In-Conversation-With-Dr--Larry-Rosen-ev0g42

21. **3.5 million public school teachers:** PBS NewsHour, April 14, 2021.

22. **"we are at an inflection point":** Conversation with Thomas Barta on the Sustainability in Action virtual panel, January 12, 2021.

Chapter 3: Singapore Slings Covid

1. **blamed for prematurely aging:** *Haze and Premature Skin Ageing,* The Straits Times, September 29, 2019, https://www.straitstimes.com/lifestyle/haze-and-premature-skin-ageing

2. **when Covid entered Singapore:** *Why Covid-19 Could Complicate Haze Prevention,* Gan Meixi and Aaron Choo, The Straits Times, July 27, 2020, https://www.straitstimes.com/opinion/why-covid-19-could-complicate-haze-prevention

3. **"the Singapore spirit at work":** *Parliament: Teary-eyed Lawrence Wong Pays Tribute to Front-Line Workers and Other Unsung Heroes in Coronavirus Fight,* Lim Yan Liang, The Straits Times, March 25, 2020, https://www.straitstimes.com/politics/singapore-coronavirus-task-force-chief-lawrence-wong-weeps-in-parliament

4. **supports only 5.7 million people:** Department of Statistics Singapore, May 2021, https://www.singstat.gov.sg/modules/infographics/populationThe Government of Singapore counts the population as at June 2020 at 5.69 million. The total number of citizens and permanent residents at that time was 4.04 million.

5. **one Hong Kong tycoon:** *Exclusive: Hong Kong Tycoons Start Moving Assets Offshore as Fears Rise Over New Extradition Law,* Greg Torode, Reuters, June 14, 2019, https://www.reuters.com/article/us-hongkong-extradition-capitalflight-ex-idUSKCN1TF1DZ

6. **Singapore's S$4 trillion:** *Singapore's asset management industry expands by 15.7%: MAS,* The Straits Times, October 1, 2020, https://www.straitstimes.com/business/economy/singapores-asset-management-industry-expands-by-157-mas

7. **foreign currency reserve:** *Official Foreign Reserves,* Monetary Authority of Singapore, April 7, 2021, https://www.mas.gov.sg/statistics/reserve-statistics/official-foreign-reserves

8. **it could also afford:** *Singapore Coronavirus Disease 2019 (Covid-19) Situation Report Weekly Report,* World Health Organization, November 8, 2020, https://www.who.int/docs/default-source/wpro---documents/countries/singapore/singapore-situation-report/covid19-sitrep-sgp-20201108.pdf?sfvrsn=c4c483ea_4

9. **swabbed by early November:** *Singapore Coronavirus Disease 2019 (Covid-19) Situation Report Weekly Report,* World Health Organization, November 8, 2020, https://www.who.int/docs/default-source/wpro---documents/countries/singapore/singapore-situation-report/covid19-sitrep-sgp-20201108.pdf?sfvrsn=c4c483ea_4

10. **dismissed at the time:** Aloysius Pang: 4th SAF Training Fatality in 18 Months, Channel News Asia, January 24, 2019, https://www.channelnewsasia.com/news/singapore/aloysius-pang-saf-training-related-death-in-18-months-mindef-11160364

11. **"such a cosy place":** Senior Minister Lee Kuan Yew's interview with Michael Bociurkiw of Forbes Magazine on 29 June, 1995, Istana, https://www.nas.gov.sg/archivesonline/data/pdfdoc/015-1995-06-29.pdf

12. **in late March 2020:** *Parliament: Teary-eyed Lawrence Wong Pays Tribute to Front-Line Workers and Other Unsung Heroes in Coronavirus Fight,* Lim Yan Liang, The Straits Times, March 25, 2020, https://www.straitstimes.com/politics/singapore-coronavirus-task-force-chief-lawrence-wong-weeps-in-parliament

13. **"Singapore needs strong men and women":** *PAP Ministers are a Pathetic Lot Who Cry in Parliament When Confronted With the Ugly Truth of Their Incompetence, Says PV Chief Lim Tean,* Online Citizen, Stephen Netto, September 2, 2020, https://www.theonlinecitizen.com/2020/09/02/pap-ministers-are-a-pathetic-lot-who-cry-in-parliament-when-confronted-with-the-ugly-truth-of-their-incompetence-says-pv-chief-lim-tean/

14. **Lee carved out a US\$30 billion:** *Singapore Industrial Park Flounders: A Deal Sours in China,* The New York Times, October 1, 1999, https://www.nytimes.com/1999/10/01/business/worldbusiness/IHT-singapore-industrial-park-flounders-a-deal-sours.html

15. **eventually Lee's estate:** *Introduction: Singapore-Suzhou Industrial Park 20 Years On: Development and Changes,* John Wong and Lye Liang Fook, World Scientific, October 2019, https://www.worldscientific.com/doi/pdf/10.1142/9789811200045_0001

16. **misfired experiment in China is mostly an anomaly:** Singapore's Direct Investment Abroad, Singapore Government, https://data.gov.sg/dataset/singapore-s-direct-investment-abroad-by-country-region-stock-as-at-year-end-annual?resource_id=421d24ed-93d7-494d-b83c-8e223915a97c

17. **it is the largest source of foreign investment:** *Myanmar's Biggest Foreign Investor Is Singapore. Here's Why That Matters,* Vice, February 18, 2021, https://www.vice.com/en/article/jgq984/myanmars-biggest-foreign-investor-is-singapore-heres-why-that-matters

18. **CCTV cameras were placed:** *Singapore's Nightclubs and Karaoke Outlets in the Dark After Pilot Fails to Take Off,* Straits Times, January 31, 2021, https://www.straitstimes.com/singapore/consumer/nightclubs-and-karaoke-outlets-in-the-dark-after-pilot-project-fails-to-take-off

19. **world's best airline:** *Our Awards,* Singapore Airlines, 2021, https://www.singaporeair.com/en_UK/sg/flying-withus/our-story/awards/

20. **created a Facebook group:** Getting Back Home to SG Facebook group, https://www.facebook.com/groups/541094413507820

21. **in a quirky twist of fate:** *Western Expatriates are Leaving Asia,* The Economist, December 16, 2020, https://www.economist.com/asia/2020/12/19/western-expatriates-are-leaving-asia

22. **had [the Trump] administration implemented:** *What the US Can Learn From Singapore's Coronavirus Strategy,* CNN Opinion, March 13, 2020, https://www.cnn.com/2020/03/13/opinions/coronavirus-what-the-us-can-learn-from-singapore-hk-bociurkiw/index.html

23. **we now know:** *Grace Assembly Coronavirus Mystery Solved: Antibody Tests Linked Mega Cluster to 2 Wuhan Tourists via CNY Party and Life Church Cluster in World First,* Timothy Got and Red Kurohi, February 26, 2020, https://www.straitstimes.com/singapore/grace-assembly-coronavirus-mystery-solved-mega-cluster-linked-to-2-wuhan-tourists-via-a

24. **didn't just block travel:** *Singapore Urges Citizens to Sign Up for Covid-19 Tracking App,* Nikkei Asia, Kentaro Iwamoto and Mayuko Tani, March 20, 2020, https://asia.nikkei.com/Spotlight/Coronavirus/Singapore-urges-citizens-to-sign-up-for-COVID-19-tracking-app

25. **for instance anyone:** *Singapore Reports 6 New Covid-19 Cases; 3 Linked to SAFRA Jurong Cluster,* Afifah Darke, March 10, 2020, https://www.channelnewsasia.com/news/singapore/coronavirus-singapore-covid19-new-cases-safra-mar-10-12521660

26. **officials admitted:** Singapore Reveals Covid Privacy Data Available to Police, BBC News, January 5, 2021, https://www.bbc.com/news/world-asia-55541001

27. **government was thrown:** *How One Singapore Sales Conference Spread Coronavirus Around the World,* Wall Street Journal, February 21, 2020, https://www.wsj.com/articles/how-one-singapore-sales-conference-spread-coronavirus-around-the-world-11582299129

28. **once the virus got out:** data provided by Ministry of Manpower, Singapore.

29. **in the fog of war:** *PM Lee says Govt must learn from errors of Covid-19 response but right decisions not always possible 'in fog of*

war,' Today Online, September 2, 2020, https://www.todayonline.com/singapore/govt-must-learn-errors-covid-19-response-right-decisions-not-always-possible-fog-war-pm

30. **growing presence:** *Singapore Opposition Make 'Landmark' Election Gains,* BBC News, May 9, 2011, https://www.bbc.com/news/world-asia-pacific-13313695

31. **visitor entry into hotspots:** *Coronavirus: Last digit of IC to Determine Entry to Four Markets,* The Straits Times, April 21, 2020, https://www.straitstimes.com/singapore/coronavirus-last-digit-of-identity-card-number-to-determine-entry-to-four-markets

32. **by early 2021:** *Coronavirus World Map: Tracking the Global Outbreak,* The New York Times, April 10, 2021, https://www.nytimes.com/interactive/2020/world/coronavirus-maps.html

33. **neighbouring Malaysia:** In May 2021, the Malaysian government imposed a third lockdown. The move was particularly controversial coming on the eve of *Hari Raya* (the end of Ramadan) festival. Internal travel, house gatherings and indoor eating was banned. See: *Malaysia Govt Defends Covid-19 Response Amid Criticism as Third Lockdown Looms,* Straits Times, May 11, 2021, https://www.straitstimes.com/asia/se-asia/malaysian-govt-defends-covid-19-response-amid-criticism-as-third-lockdown-looms

34. **by late May 2021:** A new surge in cases in May 2021 prompted the Singapore government to re-impose restrictions but stopped short of intense contact tracing along previous "circuit breaker" models. See: *Singapore Imposes 21-day Quarantine on Most Travellers, Closes Gyms to Manage Flare-up in Covid-19 Cases,* South China Morning Post, May 4, 2021, https://www.scmp.com/week-asia/health-environment/article/3132235/singapore-imposes-21-day-quarantine-most-travellers

35. **sitting down with Bloomberg TV:** Bloomberg Balance of Power, March 13, 2020, https://youtu.be/Xzzv6263sr8

36. **it had already created:** *e-Conomy SEA 2020. Resilient and Racing Ahead: Southeast Asia at Full Velocity,* November 10, 2020, Google, Temasek and Bain & Company, https://www.bain.com/insights/e-conomy-sea-2020/

37. **as 2020 ended:** *Singapore Sees Light at end of Tunnel, But PM*

Lee Hsien Loong says Virus Battle Note Yet Won, The Standard, December 31, 2020, https://www.thestandard.com.hk/breaking-news/section/6/162357/Singapore-sees-light-at-end-of-tunnel,-but-PM-Lee-Hsien-Loong-says-virus-battle-not-yet-won

38. **by late May 2021:** *Updates on Covid-19 Local Situation,* Ministry of Health Singapore, April 2021, https://www.moh.gov.sg/covid-19

39. **stabilisation's plans:** *Policy Responses to Covid-19,* International Monetary Fund, April 6, 2021, https://www.imf.org/en/Topics/imf-and-covid19/Policy-Responses-to-COVID-19#S

40. **as of February 2021:** *Pilot for Quarantine-free Business Travel Delayed Until at Least Feb 21: Sources,* Straits Times, Kok Yufeng, February 9, 2021, https://www.straitstimes.com/singapore/pilot-for-quarantine-free-business-travel-delayed-until-at-least-feb-21-sources

41. **the still raging pandemic:** *Shangri-La Dialogue in Singapore Cancelled Amid Uncertain COVID-19 Situation,* Channel News Asia, May 20, 2021, https://www.channelnewsasia.com/news/singapore/shangri-la-dialogue-singapore-cancelled-uncertain-covid-19-14848814

Chapter 4: Covid-19:
China's Chornobyl Moment

1. **trickling details:** *Turning the Pages Back: April 26, 1986, The Ukrainian Weekly,* April 24, 2015, https://www.ukrweekly.com/uwwp/april-26-1986/

2. **two days after the accident:** *Forsmark: How Sweden Alerted the World About the Danger of the Chernobyl Disaster,* European Parliament, May 15, 2014, https://www.europarl.europa.eu/news/en/headlines/society/20140514STO47018/forsmark-how-sweden-alerted-the-world-about-the-danger-of-chernobyl-disaster

3. **estimates from sources:** *"Nuclear disaster in Ukraine, Up to 15,000 feared dead,"* The Ukrainian Weekly, May 4, 1986, https://www.ukrweekly.com/uwwp/april-26-1986/

4. **decades later:** *The Chernobyl Disaster May Have Also Built a Paradise,* Wired, May 13, 2019, https://www.wired.com/story/

the-chernobyl-disaster-might-have-also-built-a-paradise/

5. **"hard for the young generation"**: *The Real Chernobyl,* SKY News, June 18, 2019, https://www.youtube.com/ watch?v=Xw3SFOfbR84&t=2626s

6. **Dr Li Wenliang:** *China's Hero Doctor was Punished for Telling the Truth About Coronavirus,* Michael Bociurkiw, CNN Opinion, February 11, 2020, https://www.cnn.com/2020/02/08/ opinions/coronavirus-bociurkiw/index.html

7. **punishing or intimidating:** *Record Number of Journalists Jailed Worldwide,* Committee to Protect Journalists, December 15, 2020, https://cpj.org/reports/2020/12/ record-number-journalists-jailed-imprisoned/

8. **go ahead with the annual:** *China's Coronavirus Response is Questioned: 'Everyone was Blindly Optimistic,'* Wall Street Journal, January 24, 2020, https://www.wsj.com/articles/ china-contends-with-questions-over-response-to-viral-out-break-11579825832

9. **delayed by about two weeks:** *Advance Team of WHO Experts Arrives in China to Probe Coronavirus,* Reuters, February 10, 2020, https://www.reuters.com/article/ us-china-health-who-idUSKBN2041S9

10. **Chinese citizens had for years:** *Chinese Tourists: Dispelling the Myths - An In-depth Look at China's Outbound Tourist Market,* McKinsey & Co., September 2018, https://www.mckinsey.com/~/ media/mckinsey/industries/travel%20transport%20and%20 logistics/our%20insights/huanying%20to%20the%20new%20 chinese%20traveler/chinese-tourists-dispelling-the-myths.ashx

11. **Covid-19 had sickened:** Johns Hopkins Coronavirus Resource Center, https://coronavirus.jhu.edu/map.html

12. **China's 'Chornobyl' moment:** The Independent Panel for Pandemic Preparedness and Response set up by the WHO described Covid-19 as the 21st century's 'Chernobyl moment' and said the WHO should have declared a global emergency much earlier. See: https://theindependentpanel.org/wp-content/ uploads/2021/05/COVID-19-Make-it-the-Last-Pandemic_final.pdf

13. **offered China a chance:** *Geopolitics and the Vaccines,* Oxford Analytica webinar, March 17, 2021, https://www.oxan.com/

insights/webinars-and-events/calls/deep-dive-webinar-march/

14. **turned its entire country:** *China Prepares Large-Scale Rollout of Coronavirus Vaccines,* ABC News, December 6, 2020, https://abcnews.go.com/Health/wireStory/ china-prepares-large-scale-rollout-covid-19-vaccines-74565366

15. **stem cell technology:** *Scientists Use Stem Cells to Treat Covid-19 Patients in China,* IEEE Spectrum, March 26, 2019, https://spectrum.ieee.org/the-human-os/biomedical/devices/ stem-cells-covid19-china

16. **"be transparent":** Tweet by China Foreign Ministry spokesperson Lijian Zhao, March 12, 2021, https://twitter.com/zlj517/ status/1238111898828066823?s=20

17. **one could make an informed guess:** *Why Putin Wants to Keep Navalny Locked Up,* Michael Bociurkiw, CNN Opinion, January 19, 2021, https://www.cnn.com/2021/01/19/opinions/ navalny-putin-russia-arrest-bociurkiw/index.html

18. **Kremlin tried to hide:** *What Really Happened to Russia's 'Unsinkable' Sub,* Martin Bright, The Guardian, August 5, 2001, https://www.theguardian.com/world/2001/aug/05/kursk.russia

19. **"this type of authoritarian":** interview with Michael Vatikiotis for The Frontline Club, February 23, 2021

20. **some estimates suggest:** *China is Installing Surveillance Cameras Outside People's Front Doors…and Sometimes Inside Their Homes,* CNN, April 28, 2020, https://www.cnn.com/2020/04/27/ asia/cctv-cameras-china-hnk-intl/index.html

21. **assigns social credit scores:** *The Rise of Digital Authoritarianism,* Freedom House, 2018, https://freedomhouse. org/report/freedom-net/2018/rise-digital-authoritarianism

22. **Chinese technicians were reportedly:** *Burmese Expert: China Helping Military Establish Cyber Firewall* , Voice of America, February 12, 2021, https://www.voanews.com/east-asia-pacific/ burmese-expert-china-helping-military-establish-cyber-firewall

23. **made in China 2025:** *Is 'Made in China 2025' a Threat to Global Trade?,* Council on Foreign Relations, May 13, 2019, https://www. cfr.org/backgrounder/made-china-2025-threat-global-trade

24. **"in late 2020 Xi devoted":** *China's Xi Jinping is Pushing for a*

Global Covid QR Code. He May Struggle to Convince the World,
CNN, November 23, 2020, https://www.cnn.com/2020/11/23/asia/
china-xi-qr-code-coronavirus-intl-hnk/index.html

25. **"debt trap diplomacy":** *Remarks by Vice President Pence on
the Administration's Policy Towards China,* The Trump White
House, October 4, 2018, https://trumpwhitehouse.archives.gov/
briefings-statements/remarks-vice-president-pence-administra-
tions-policy-toward-china/

26. **"setting global standards":** Interview with Michael Popow,
March 31, 2021

27. **state subsidies:** *Is 'Made in China 2025 a Threat to Global
Trade?,* Council on Foreign Relations, May 13, 2019, https://www.
cfr.org/backgrounder/made-china-2025-threat-global-trade

28. **result:** from my Global Impact podcast interview with Jennifer Zhu Scott, June 2, 2020,
https://anchor.fm/michael-bociurkiw/episodes/
Episode-13-In-Conversation-with-Jennifer-Zhu-Scott-ees5d3

29. **DXY is a company to watch:** *Chinese online Health
Platform DXY Closes $500M Raise,* Mobile Health News,
January 4, 2021, https://www.mobihealthnews.com/news/
chinese-online-health-platform-dxy-closes-500m-raise

30. **the average Chinese person:** from my Global
Impact podcast interview with Jennifer Zhu Scott, June
2, 2020, https://anchor.fm/michael-bociurkiw/episodes/
Episode-13-In-Conversation-with-Jennifer-Zhu-Scott-ees5d3

31. **a report by Boston Consulting Group:** *Sharp Growth
Likely for Online Healthcare Sector in China, China Daily,*
August 11, 2020, https://www.chinadaily.com.cn/a/202008/11/
WS5f31f59ea31083481725f80f.html

32. **online drugs sales:** *China's Changing Pharmaceutical E-commerce
Market,* Deloitte, 2016, https://www2.deloitte.com/content/dam/
Deloitte/de/Documents/life-sciences-health-care/Chinas_chang-
ing_pharmaceutical_ECommerce_Market.pdf

33. **by early 2021:** Oxford Analytica webinar 'Geopolitics and the
Vaccine, March 17, 2021.

34. **according to one projection:** By May 21, 2021, 483 million
doses had been administered in China, according to the Johns

Hopkins Coronavirus Resource Center. See: *Coronavirus: China Piles on the Pressure to get Vaccinated as Country Targets 10 Million Injections a Day,* South China Morning Post, March 26, 2021, https://www.scmp.com/news/china/science/article/3127166/coronavirus-china-piles-pressure-get-vaccinated-country-targets

35. **"remembered":** Oxford Analytica webinar 'Geopolitics and the Vaccine, March 17, 2021.

36. **by comparison:** By May 21, 2021, only 7.1% of the Russians had been fully vaccinated, according to *The New York Times.* See: *Russia Beat the World to a Vaccine, so Why is it Falling Behind on Vaccinations?,* The New Yorker, April 12, 2021, https://www.newyorker.com/news/daily-comment/russia-beat-the-world-to-a-vaccine-so-why-is-it-falling-behind-on-vaccinations

37. **Sputnik V was eventually shipped:** *Russia is Offering to Export Hundreds of Millions of Vaccine Doses But Can it Deliver?,* Andrew Kramer, New York Times, February 19, 2021, https://www.nytimes.com/2021/02/19/world/europe/russia-coronavirus-vaccine-soft-power.htmlThis article states more than 50 countries ordered 1.2 billion doses of the Russian vaccine

38. **"it's just naive":** interview with Dr. Nahid Bhadelia, March 8, 2021. On May 10, 2021, the Director General of the WHO slammed producing nations for using vaccine diplomacy, calling it "geopolitical manoeuvring." See: https://www.michaelbociurkiw.com/news/2021/5/10/covid-who-vaccines

39. **according to the coalition:** *Meeting Discusses Covid-19 Vaccine Manufacturing Bottlenecks That Must be Urgently Tackled for Covid-19 Vaccine Output to Reach its Full Potential,* Coalition for Epidemic Preparedness Innovations (CEPI). March 9, 2021, https://cepi.net/news_cepi/meeting-discusses-covid-19-vaccine-manufacturing-bottlenecks-that-must-be-urgently-tackled-for-covid-19-vaccine-output-to-reach-its-full-potential/

40. **two-thirds of the world's advanced:** *Analysis: Money no Object as Governments Race to Build Chip Arsenals,* Reuters, March 26, 2021, https://www.reuters.com/article/us-usa-semiconductors-subsidies-idUKKBN2BI1CY

41. **made in Taiwan:** *TSMC Gears up for Mass Production of 3-nanometre Chips for High-End Computers and 5G Phones,* South China Morning Post, January 18, 2021, https://www.scmp.com/tech/

innovation/article/3118183/tsmc-gears-mass-production-3-nano-metre-chips-high-end-computers-and

42. **a top US officer:** *China Threat to Invade Taiwan is 'Closer Than Most Think', says US Admiral,* The Guardian, March 23, 2021, https://www.theguardian.com/world/2021/mar/23/taiwan-china-threat-admiral-john-aquilino

43. **a huge population:** *China's Policies on Stem Cell Research: An Opportunity for International Collaborations,* Nature, October, 2008, https://www.nature.com/articles/nrm2528-c1.pdf?origin=ppub

44. **group of seven patients:** *Coronavirus: Critically Ill Chinese Patient Saved by Stem Cell Therapy, Study Says,* South China Morning Post, March 2, 2020, https://www.scmp.com/news/china/society/article/3053080/coronavirus-critically-ill-chinese-patient-saved-stem-cell

45. **including the University of Miami:** *University of Miami Leads Groundbreaking Trial for Covid-19 Treatment,* Eurek Alert, January 5, 2021, https://www.eurekalert.org/pub_releases/2021-01/uomm-uom010421.php

Chapter 5: Covid-19 Crushes Diplomacy, Just When We Needed It

1. **protocols on international travel:** *WHO Chief says Widespread Travel Bans not Needed to Beat China Virus,* Reuters, February 3, 2020, https://www.reuters.com/article/us-china-health-who-idUSKBN1ZX1H3

2. **vaccine passports:** *WHO Does not Back Vaccination Passports for Now – Spokeswoman,* Reuters, April 6, 2021, https://www.reuters.com/article/us-health-coronavirus-who-vaccines-idUSKBN2BT158

3. **journalist and war correspondent:** *America Shows Troubling Warning Signs of a Slide Into Civil War,* Janine di Giovanni, Medium, October 26, 2020, https://medium.com/@janinedigiovanni

4. **"repeatedly":** Dr. Syra Madad quoted in my CNN Opinion

OpEd, December 2, 2020, https://www.cnn.com/2020/12/02/opinions/justin-trudeau-covid-19-vaccine-crisis-bociurkiw/index.html

5. **"not ready for the next pandemic"**: Bill Gates Notes, March 18, 2015, https://www.gatesnotes.com/health/we-are-not-ready-for-the-next-epidemic

6. **"this could've been worse"**: Bill Gates on PBS NewsHour, February 22, 2021, https://twitter.com/NewsHour/status/1364061672789393408?s=20

7. **iconic photo:** *The Already Iconic G7 Photo is a Trump Rorschach Test*, Chris Chillizza, CNN, June 11, 2018, https://www.cnn.com/2018/06/11/politics/g7-photo

8. **tantrum diplomacy:** *At the G20, Those who Yelled the Loudest Were Heard*, Michael Bociurkiw, CNN Opinion, June 30, 2019, https://www.cnn.com/2019/06/30/opinions/g20-osaka-tantrum-diplomacy-saudi-arabia-china-russia-bociurkiw

9. **Twitter eventually began:** *President Trump Permanently Banned From Twitter Over Risk He Could Incite Violence*, USA Today, January 8, 2021, https://www.usatoday.com/story/tech/2021/01/08/twitter-permanently-bans-president-trump/6603578002/

10. **when Petro Poroshenko was elected:** Years later, the chief of staff of his successor, the TV comedian-turned actor Volodymyr Zelensky, reportedly tried to organize a high-level visit to the U.S. Capitol by by-passing the Ukrainian Embassy in Washington, D.C., going instead through a wealthy US-based Ukrainian businessman. See Tweet by @worldaffairspro, May 19, 2021, https://twitter.com/WorldAffairsPro/status/1395138362357338113?s=20

11. **middle of a pandemic:** *The Conflict we Can't Ignore*, Michael Bociurkiw, CNN Opinion, October 13, 2020, https://www.cnn.com/2020/10/13/opinions/nagorno-karabakh-conflict-we-cant-ignore-bociurkiw/index.html

12. **entourages:** *Mugabe Family on Spending Spree as Dad 'Naps' at UN General Assembly*, Africa News, September 20, 2017, https://www.africanews.com/2017/09/20/mugabe-family-on-spending-spree-as-dad-naps-at-un-general-assembly//

13. **technological train wreck:** *Is China the New Leader on the World Health Stage?*, Michael Bociurkiw, CNN Opinion, May 20, 2020, https://www.cnn.com/2020/05/20/opinions/

world-health-assembly-xi-trump-bociurkiw/index.html

14. **"personal contact is an essential"**: *Press Conference by Secretary-General António Guterres at United Nations Headquarters*, UN website, September 16, 2020, https://www.un.org/press/en/2020/sgsm20258.doc.htm

15. **"still a work in progress"**: ICRC President Peter Mauer in conversation with Michael Bociurkiw on Global Impact podcast, October 2, 2020, https://anchor.fm/michael-bociurkiw/episodes/S2-E5-In-Conversation-with-Peter-Maurer--ICRC-ekfnta

16. **ICRC-brokered prisoner swap**: *Yemen War: Houthis and Government Complete Prisoner Exchange*, BBC News, October 16, 2020, https://www.bbc.com/news/world-middle-east-54552051

17. **"face-to-face meetings are critical"**: Statement of the Co-Chairs of the Geneva International Discussions, UN website, October 6, 2020, https://dppa.un.org/en/statement-of-co-chairs-of-geneva-international-discussions-2

18. **"what worries me"**: Michael Vatikiotis on Frontline Club virtual panel, February 25, 2021, https://www.youtube.com/watch?v=IY0D71nJ9as&t=402s

19. **"giving materials"**: Conversation With Philippe Moreau Chevrolet on the Global Impact Podcast, March 25, 2020 https://anchor.fm/michael-bociurkiw/episodes/In-Conversation-With-Philippe-Moreau-Chevrolet-etgg6h

20. **people ruled by a junta**: *What Could Make Myanmar's Military Junta Back Off?*, CNN Opinion, Michael Bociurkiw, March 9, 2021, https://www.cnn.com/2021/03/08/opinions/myanmar-diplomacy-military-junta-bociurkiw/index.html

21. **claim overlapping ownership**: *White House Warns China on Growing Militarization in South China Sea*, CNN, May 4, 2018, https://www.cnn.com/2018/05/03/asia/south-china-sea-missiles-spratly-intl/index.html

22. **Covid-19 was used as an excuse**: *Trinidad's 2020 Elections and Covid-19*, August 6, 2020, https://theglobalamericans.org/2020/08/trinidads-2020-elections-and-covid-19/

23. **EU leaders**: The World This Week, France 24, December 18, 2020, https://www.france24.com/en/tv-shows/the-world-this-week/20201218-macron-contracts-covid-biden-wins-again-nige-

rian-schoolboys-freed-remembering-john-le-carr%C3%A9

24. **"good luck in contact tracing":** Ibid.

25. **warnings about the coronavirus:** *Taiwan Says It Tried to Warn the World About Coronavirus. Here's What It Really Knew and When,* Time, May 19, 2020, https://time.com/5826025/taiwan-who-trump-coronavirus-covid19/

26. **"whoever screams the loudest":** *At the G20, Those who Yelled the Loudest Were Heard,* Michael Bociurkiw, CNN Opinion, June 30, 2019, https://www.cnn.com/2019/06/30/opinions/g20-osaka-tan-trum-diplomacy-saudi-arabia-china-russia-bociurkiw

27. **2018 APEC meeting:** Ibid.

Chapter 6: Covid-19, Digital Divides, Selfies and Influencers

1. **digital canyon:** *Two Thirds of the World's School-age Children Have no Internet Access at Home, new UNICEF-ITU Report Says,* November, 2020, https://www.unicef.org/press-releases/two-thirds-worlds-school-age-children-have-no-internet-access-home-new-unicef-itu

2. **research conducted in 2018:** *Internet/Broadband Fact Sheet,* Pew Research Centre, April, 2021, https://www.pewresearch.org/internet/fact-sheet/internet-broadband/?menuItem=2ab2b-0be-6364-4d3a-8db7-ae134dbc05cd

3. **five million US households:** *The Numbers Behind the Broadband 'Homework Gap,* Pew Research Center, April 20, 2015, https://www.pewresearch.org/fact-tank/2015/04/20/the-numbers-behind-the-broadband-homework-gap/

4. **US cities and school districts:** *Using School Bus WiFi to Support Distance Learning, School Transportation News,* May 1, 2020, https://stnonline.com/partner-updates/using-school-bus-wifi-to-support-distance-learning/

5. **plenty of studies:** *WiFi-equipped School Buses Help Students get Online,* CNN, October 21, 2017, https://www.cnn.com/2017/10/31/tech/homework-gap/index.html

6. **the problems can get worse:** *Two Thirds of the World's School-age Children Have no Internet Access at Home, new UNICEF-ITU Report Says,* UNICEF press release, November, 2020, https://www.unicef.org/press-releases/two-thirds-worlds-school-age-children-have-no-internet-access-home-new-unicef-itu

7. **in March 2021:** *One Year into the Pandemic, a New Survey Reveals That Teens and Young Adults Are Actively Turning to Online Sources to Cope with Mental Health,* Common Sense Media, March 17, 2021, https://www.commonsensemedia.org/about-us/news/press-releases/one-year-into-the-pandemic-a-new-survey-reveals-that-teens-and-young

8. **"used for great things":** *Coping with Covid-19: How Young People Use Digital Media to Manage Their Mental Health,* Common Sense Media, March 17, 2021, https://www.youtube.com/watch?v=sJwNR3usjz4

9. **"young people's mental health needs":** Ibid.

10. **1.4 trillion photos:** *Our Best Photos Deserve to be Printed,* Key Point Intelligence, December, 2018, https://www.keypointintelligence.com/news/editors-desk/2018/september/our-best-photos-deserve-to-be-printed/

11. **measly 380 million photos:** *How Many Photos Have Been Taken Ever?,* BuzzFeed, September 24, 2012, https://www.buzzfeed.com/hunterschwarz/how-many-photos-have-been-taken-ever-6zgv

12. **"Everybody is taking selfies":** *Social Media Firms Must Protect Children - or Face new Laws, says Jeremy Hunt,* SKY News, April 22, 2018, https://ca.sports.yahoo.com/news/social-media-firms-must-protect-children-face-laws-030800721.html

13. **"it looks like I am in Bali":** post on Instagram, https://www.instagram.com/explore/tags/siberianmaldives/

14. **before the pandemic:** Instagram post of 'Gates of Heaven' by @ggworldwide, January 15, 2020, https://www.instagram.com/p/B7Wn01Nh_HY/?igshid=eg2hoslv4zfg

15. **sneaky mirror:** Instagram post by @iphonetravelpictures, June, 2020, https://www.instagram.com/p/CBXKWnusVGL/?utm_source=ig_web_copy_link

16. **Abigail Posner:** interview with Michael Bociurkiw, March 2020.

17. **"decorum":** *Rome's New Rules: No Sitting on the Spanish Steps (and No Wading into the Trevi Fountain),* New York Times, August 7, 2019, https://www.nytimes.com/2019/08/07/world/europe/rome-spanish-steps-sit.html

18. **rude kids:** Ibid.

19. **advertisements:** *New Zealand Urges People to Ditch Influencer-Style Tourism Photos,* BBC News, January 20, 2021, https://www.bbc.com/news/world-asia-55827641

20. **reopening tourist flights:** *Australia Opens Travel Bubble With New Zealand,* BBC News, April 20, 2021, https://www.bbc.com/news/world-australia-56796679

21. **another tourist site swamped:** *Crowds, Backed-up Traffic Force Closure of Poppy Viewing Area in Lake Elsinore,* Mercury News, March 17, 2019, https://www.mercurynews.com/2019/03/17/crowds-traffic-congestion-prompt-lake-elsinore-to-shut-down-poppy-viewing/

22. **Jaci Marie Smith:** Instagram post by Jaci Marie Smith, March 1, 2019, https://www.instagram.com/p/Buenb-snJOX/?igshid=1mbfkmytqnzxj

23. **Gulin Cetin:** Instagram account, https://www.instagram.com/gulincetin/?hl=en

24. **California's Big Sur:** *Big Sur is Fed up With 'Selfie Tourism.' Here's its New Plan to Transform Travel in the Region,* San Francisco Chronicle, December 30, 2020, https://www.sfchronicle.com/travel/article/New-Big-Sur-plan-aims-to-control-tourists-at-15836501.php

25. **in the year of 2020:** *International Tourist Arrivals Reach 1.4 Billion Two Years Ahead Of Forecasts,* World Tourism Organization, January 21, 2019, https://bit.ly/3vdPrMP

26. **travel contributed:** *Economic Impact Report,* World Travel and Tourism Council, 2020, https://wttc.org/Research/Economic-Impact

27. **out-of-control:** Overtourism Mapped: Tourism is Headed Into a Global Crisis, Responsible Tourism, 2019, https://www.responsibletravel.com/copy/overtourism-map

28. **"ways to balance"**: interview with Monica Bormetti.

29. **"not to hold a crayon"**: interview with Monica Bormetti, July 12, 2018.

30. **"means a drastic shift"**: interview with Imran Chaudhri, August, 2018.

31. **"100% heroin"**: Elspeth Day post on A Small World discussion, January 11, 2018.

32. **best advice**: A 2017 UNICEF report on children and technology argued that parents and caregivers are best to monitor what their children do on devices, rather track time spent online. It said: "there is no clear agreement on when time spent on digital technology shifts from moderate to excessive; 'how much is too much' is highly individual, dependent on a child's age, individual characteristics and broader life context...More attention should be given to the content and activities of children's digital experiences rather than to how much time they spend in front of screens." See: *Children in a Digital World*, https://www.unicef.org/media/48601/file

33. **L'Oreal brand ambassador**: Instagram post by Eva Longoria, May 1, 2020, https://www.instagram.com/tv/B_prHBnJ1HZ/?utm_source=ig_embed

34. **online mental health providers**: *How Covid-19 Is Changing The Game For Travel Influencers*, Forbes, June 9, 2020, https://www.forbes.com/sites/adriennejordan/2020/06/09/how-covid-19-is-changing-the-game-for-travel-influencers/?sh=374fb5632f4a

35. **nano influencer:** *The 2020 Influencer Pricing Report*, Klear, November 11, 2020, https://klear.com/blog/the-2020-influencer-pricing-report/

36. **survey by social intelligence platform**: Ibid.

37. **Klear survey found women**: Ibid.

38. **pay gap**: *Women Make up Majority of Influencer Community, Still Earn Less Than Male Influencers*, Marketing Land, January 6, 2019, https://marketingland.com/women-make-up-majority-of-influencer-community-earn-less-than-male-influencers-262193

39. **"a heavy dose of sex appeal"**: Ibid.

40. **stand next to a BMW**: Ibid.

41. **international tourist arrivals:** *OECD Tourism Trends and Policies 2020,* OECD, 2020, https://www.oecd.org/cfe/tourism/OECD-Tourism-Trends-Policies%202020-Highlights-ENG.pdf

42. **double their spending:** *Influencer Marketing: Social Media Influencer Market Stats and Research for 2021,* Business Insider, January 6, 2021, https://www.businessinsider.com/influencer-marketing-report

43. **brands now focus much more on Gen Z:** *State of Influencer Marketing 2021,* Klear Research, 2020, https://klear.com/2021-state-of-influencer-marketing.pdf

44. **getting little ROI:** *ROI Evaluation and Fake Followers are Making Brands Struggle in Measuring Influencer Attribution,* Digital Transformation World, June 1, 2019, https://www.digitalinformationworld.com/2019/06/roi-measurement-and-fake-followers-marketing.html#

45. **high number of followers:** *How Covid-19 Is Changing The Game For Travel Influencers,* Forbes, June 9, 2020, https://www.forbes.com/sites/adriennejordan/2020/06/09/how-covid-19-is-changing-the-game-for-travel-influencers/?sh=374fb5632f4a

46. **new paid partnership feature:** *How and Why to Use the Paid Partnership Feature on Instagram,* Business 2 Community, February 1, 2020, https://www.business2community.com/instagram/how-and-why-to-use-the-paid-partnership-feature-on-instagram-02280127

47. **pressure from the US Federal Trade Commission:** *FTC Cracking Down on Social Influencers' Labeling of Paid Promotions,* Ad Age, August 5, 2016, https://adage.com/article/digital/ftc-cracking-social-influencers-labeling-promotions/305345

48. **Scott and Collette Stohler:** Instagram post by @roamaroo, April 2, 2020, https://www.instagram.com/p/CNK0WvNFxWF/?utm_source=ig_web_copy_link

49. **awaiting the resumption of flights:** Instagram post by @finduslost https://www.instagram.com/p/CGXohk5Da2K/?igshid=dh1a2i1hdcyq

50. **the day job:** Instagram profile of @travelbabbo (**194,000 followers**), https://www.instagram.com/travelbabbo/

51. **another influencer:** Instagram profile of Callum Snape (aka @ calsnape), https://www.instagram.com/calsnape/

52. **"tone deafness":** interview with Callum Snape, January 31, 2021.

53. **egregious example:** *Rod Phillips Resigns as Ontario Finance Minister Following Secret Pandemic Getaway,* CTV News, December 31, 2020, https://toronto.ctvnews.ca/rod-phillips-re-signs-as-ontario-finance-minister-following-secret-pandemic-get-away-1.5249471?cache=tljuektxk%3FclipId%3D89619

54. **esprit de corps:** interview with Shachi Kurl, April 2020.

55. **Bad Etiquette Award:** *Kim Kardashian West Mocked for 'Humble' Birthday Party on Private Island,* BBC News, October 28, 2020, https://www.bbc.com/news/world-us-canada-54714660

56. **"40 and feeling so humbled and blessed":** Tweet by Kim Kardashian, October 27, 2020, https://twitter.com/ KimKardashian/status/1321151192165134344?s=20

57. **"whatever possessed Kim Kardashian":** Tweet by @hey-itskmatt, October 27, 2020, https://twitter.com/heyitskmatt/ status/1321191929338626049?s=20

58. **"are you that insensitive":** Tweet by Peter Frampton, October 27, 2020, https://twitter.com/peterframpton/ status/1321226316327325696?s=20

59. **Vancouver-based life coach:** *Vancouver Influencer's Trip to Hawaii During Pandemic Sparks Outrage, Vancouver is Awesome,* February 9, 2021, https://www.vancouverisawesome.com/vancou-ver-news/vancouver-influencers-trip-to-hawaii-during-pandem-ic-sparks-outrage-3367216

60. **"I wasn't entirely sure":** screenshot of Tweet by Leah Brathwaite via @erin_g, February 8, 2021, https://twitter.com/ erin_gee/status/1358921809777819653/photo/1

61. **"obviously a mistake":** *Cruz Calls Cancun, Mexico, Trip 'a Mistake' as Texans Remain Without Power Amid Historic Winter Storm,* CNN, February 19, 2021, https://www.cnn.com/2021/02/18/poli-tics/ted-cruz-cancun-texas-disaster-electricity-power-water/index. html

62. **group text messages:** *Ted Cruz's Cancún Trip: Family Texts Details His Political Behaviour,* New York Times, February 19,

2021, https://www.nytimes.com/2021/02/18/us/politics/ted-cruz-storm-cancun.html

63. **"tedium into a business":** *Hilaria Baldwin is Trying to Reframe her Fake-Accent Story as an Attempt to Rescue a Victim (Herself) by a Hero (also Herself),* The Globe and Mail, January 8, 2021, https://www.theglobeandmail.com/arts/article-hilaria-baldwin-is-trying-to-reframe-her-fake-accent-story-as-an/

64. **"sometimes see people":** interview with Sue Varma, March, 2021.

65. **Hong Kong's low-cost airline:** *Controversy Over Free 'Nowhere' Flight in Hong Kong for Influencers Amid Looming Cathay Pacific job Cuts, Environmental Backlash,* South China Morning Post, October 14, 2020, https://www.scmp.com/news/hong-kong/transport/article/3105481/controversy-over-free-nowhere-flight-hong-kong-influencers

66. **"rediscover the joy of flying":** Ibid.

67. **Air Canada also leveraged influencers:** *Senior Bureaucrat Overseeing Border and Travel Health Accepted Air Canada Junket to Jamaica,* The Globe and Mail, January 7, 2021, https://www.theglobeandmail.com/politics/article-senior-bureaucrat-overseeing-border-and-travel-health-accepted-air/

68. **full-time influencer:** Instagram profile of Dominique Baker, https://www.instagram.com/dominique.baker/

69. **became hip:** *Silicon Valley is Going Crazy for Clubhouse, a Social Media App With 1500 Users That's Already Worth $100 Million,* CNBC, May 20, 2020, https://www.cnbc.com/2020/05/20/clubhouse-app-is-where-mc-hammer-and-jared-leto-chat-with-vcs.html

70. **Twitter has since introduced:** *Twitter Launches Rival Audio Chat Rooms Feature Spaces on Android,* USA Today, March 3, 2021, https://www.usatoday.com/story/tech/2021/03/03/clubhouse-rival-twitter-launches-spaces-audio-chat-room-android/6901089002/. In May 2021, Twitter launched a tip feature on Spaces.

Chapter 7: Broken News

1. **"Christ sent evil spirits":** *Breaking News*, page 2, Robert MacNeil, 1998, Knopf Doubleday Publishing Group.

2. **spouting opinions:** While Fox News, owned by the Rupert Murdoch family, was embraced opinion reporting on US politics, CNN maintained a comparatively large news schedule via its CNN International reporting and daytime programming. It maintains major news operations in Atlanta and New York City, along with major hubs in London and Hong Kong.

3. **American hedge funds swooping:** *Tribune Shareholders Vote to Sell Legendary Chain of Newspapers to a Hedge Fund*, Washington Post, May 21, 2021, https://www.washingtonpost.com/media/2021/05/21/tribune-sale-alden-hedge-fund/

4. **college dorm experiment:** *Facebook at 15: How a College Experiment Changed the World*, CNN, February 1, 2019, https://www.cnn.com/interactive/2019/02/business/facebook-history-timeline/index.html

5. **generated US$84.2 billion:** Of Facebook's US$86 billion revenue in 2020, almost 98% was from digital advertising. See: *Google, Facebook Must Pay for News: Here's Why*, Gulf News, March 2, 2021, https://gulfnews.com/special-reports/google-facebook-must-pay-for-news-heres-why-1.1614686890189

6. **measly US$800 million:** *The New York Times, Which Trump Often Derides as 'Failing,' Says 2019 Was a Record Year for Digital Growth*, CNBC, January 15, 2020, https://www.cnbc.com/2020/01/15/new-york-times-says-2019-was-a-record-year-for-digital-growth.html

7. **forced by unions:** *Daily Telegraph to Withdraw Devices Monitoring Time at Desk After Criticism*, The Guardian, January 11, 2016, https://www.theguardian.com/media/2016/jan/11/daily-telegraph-to-withdraw-devices-monitoring-time-at-desk-after-criticism

8. **ranked by "Stars":** *Daily Telegraph Plans to Link Journalists' Pay With Article Popularity*, The Guardian, March 15, 2021, https://www.theguardian.com/media/2021/mar/15/daily-telegraph-plans-link-journalists-pay-article-popularity

9. **"it's grotesque":** Ibid.

10. **another system at Fortune magazine:** Tweet by Steve Perlberg of Business Insider, March 16, 2021, https://twitter.com/perlberg/status/1371821634429014016?s=20

11. **London's City AM newspaper:** *City AM Delays Print Return as Commuter Audience Slow to Get Back Into Office,* Press Gazette, September 3, 2020, https://www.pressgazette.co.uk/city-am-delays-print-return-as-commuter-audience-slow-to-get-back-into-office/

12. **slashed editorial staff salaries:** *London Newspaper City AM Slashes Salaries By 50% As Coronavirus Keeps Readers Home,* Forbes, March 20, 2020, https://www.forbes.com/sites/isabel-togoh/2020/03/20/london-newspaper-city-am-cuts-salaries-by-50-as-coronavirus-keeps-readers-home/?sh=1195456b8bce

13. **free paper:** *Evening Standard Announces Pay Cut and Furloughs After ad Slump,* The Guardian, April 1, 2020, https://www.theguardian.com/media/2020/apr/01/evening-standard-announces-pay-cuts-and-furloughs-after-ad-slump

14. **circulation of Metro:** *Metro Continues to Print at a Loss to Serve UK's Key Workers Still Commuting,* Press Gazette, April 21, 2020, https://www.pressgazette.co.uk/metro-continues-to-print-at-a-loss-to-serve-uk-key-workers-still-commuting/

15. **journalists pulled a 24-hour strike:** *24 Hours: Editorial Employees of The New Yorker Engage in a Day-Long Work Stoppage,* The News Guild of New York, press release, January 21, 2021, https://www.nyguild.org/post/id-24-hours-editorial-employees-of-the-new-yorker-engage-in-a-day-long-work-stoppage

16. **"only apply if your parents pay your rent":** Tweet by Lindsay Crouse, January 21, 2021, https://twitter.com/lindsaycrouse/status/1352288670330531841?s=20

17. **in March 2021:** *New Yorker Staffers Vote to Authorize Strike Amid Tensions with Condé Nast,* The Guardian, March 29, 2021, https://www.theguardian.com/media/2021/mar/29/new-yorker-union-strike-conde-nast-ars-technica-pitchfork

18. **"newsrooms worldwide":** interview with Victor Malarek, March 15, 2021.

19. **Gallup poll:** *Americans' Trust in Mass Media Sinks to New*

Low, Gallup Poll, September 14, 2016, https://news.gallup.com/
poll/195542/americans-trust-mass-media-sinks-new-low.aspx

20. **"they all declined":** Tweet from NBC News PR quoting 'Meet
the Press' host Chuck Todd, November 15, 2020, https://twitter.
com/NBCNewsPR/status/1327982395237277698?s=20

21. **"here's our comment":** Tweet by CNN's Daniel
Dale, January 21, 2021, https://twitter.com/ddale8/
status/1352388098576027649?s=20

22. **The assault on the news media:** *Freedom and the Media
2019: Media Freedom: A Downward Spiral,* Freedom House, 2019,
https://freedomhouse.org/report/freedom-and-media/2019/
media-freedom-downward-spiral

23. **Indian minister:** *Presstitutes Remark Row: PM
Narendra Modi Says Media Ignoring V K Singh's Good
Work in Yemen,* The Indian Express, April 19, 2015,
https://indianexpress.com/article/india/india-others/
pm-salutes-vk-singh-slams-media-for-ignoring-good-work/

24. **worse than in India:** *In Memoriam: Journalists and
Media Workers Lost to Covid-19 in India,* Network of
Women in Media, India, May 2021, https://docs.google.
com/document/d/e/2PACX-1vTkXC1UzWBeXiz39WHro-
eqleYml9WJui-SbQIu7nANl0zjC-c0jp_maF0XeTNAqOg/
pub

25. **University of North Carolina:** *News Deserts And Ghost
Newspapers: Will Local News Survive?* the Hussman School of
Journalism and Media at the University of North Carolina at
Chapel Hill, June 2020, https://www.usnewsdeserts.com/reports/
news-deserts-and-ghost-newspapers-will-local-news-survive/
the-news-landscape-in-2020-transformed-and-diminished/

26. **round after round of layoffs:** Ibid.

27. **online media giant HuffPost:** *Layoffs Underway at HuffPost
a Day After Parent Company Verizon Announced Cuts,* CNN
Business, January 24, 2019, https://www.cnn.com/2019/01/24/
media/huffpost-layoffs/index.html

28. **enterprise health reporting section:** *Insiders:
HuffPost Layoffs Hit 20 Employees Throughout Editorial,*
The Wrap, January 24, 2019, https://www.thewrap.com/

insiders-huffpost-layoffs-hit-20-employees-throughout-editorial/

29. **BuzzFeed acquired HuffPost:** *BuzzFeed Lays off 70 HuffPost Staffers in Massive 'Restructure' Less Than a Month After Acquisition,* CNN Business, March 9, 2021, https://www.cnn.com/2021/03/09/media/huffpost-layoffs/index.html

30. *"don't judge me":* email conversation with an acquaintance in Seattle, WA, February 2021.

31. **subsidised:** *CBC Temporarily Replaces Local Evening TV News Amid Coronavirus Pandemic,* CBC, March 18, 2020, https://www.cbc.ca/news/canada/cbc-tvnews-changes-coronavirus-1.5501512

32. **systems would fail:** CBC President Catherine Tait speaking to CBC News The Current, *'We totally understand the frustration': CBC president defends local TV news suspension amid pandemic,* CBC News, March 24, 2020, https://www.cbc.ca/radio/thecurrent/the-current-for-march-24-2020-1.5507880/we-totally-understand-the-frustration-cbc-president-defends-local-tv-news-suspension-amid-pandemic-1.5508146

33. **CBC local TV news:** *Citizens Group Petitions CBC to Restore Local Newscasts,* The Georgia Straight, March 20, 2020, https://www.straight.com/news/1374786/citizens-group-petitions-cbc-restore-local-newscasts

34. **Boston marathon bombings:** *Update: Massive Citizen Smartphone Photo and Video Probe Underway into Boston Bombings,* ComputerWorld, April 16, 2013, https://www.computerworld.com/article/2496764/update--massive-citizen-smartphone-photo-and-video-probe-underway-into-boston-bombings.html

35. **horrific crash of Asiana Airlines flight 214:** *Airports: The Nature of Flight,* Christopher Schaberg, Bloombury, 2017, https://books.google.ca/books?id=1BcqDwAAQBAJ&pg=PA100&lpg=PA100&dq=asian+flight+214+images+smartphones&source=bl&ots=jXm1pbNZup&sig=ACfU3U1hc-TanQLlE2k7I5QVMEvmeEartdQ&hl=en&sa=X&ved=2ahUKEwjNq9nNn5rwAhVUPn0KHQTNB3YQ6AEwEXoECBAQAw#v=onepage&q=asian%20flight%20214%20images%20smartphones&f=false

36. **forced to admit:** *What Motivated Iran to Come Clean,* Michael

Bociurkiw, CNN Opinion, January 11, 2020, https://www.cnn.
com/2020/01/11/opinions/what-motivated-iran-to-come-clean-
bociurkiw/index.html

37. **best examples:** *36 Stories That Prove Citizen Journalism Matters,*
by Katie Hawkins-Gaar, April 23, 2013, CNN, https://www.cnn.
com/2013/04/03/opinion/ireport-awards-hawkins-gaar

38. **English teacher:** Ibid.

39. **delightful example:** Dr Clare Wenham was being interviewed by
BBC News on local lockdowns when her young daughter inter-
rupted, July 2, 2020, https://youtu.be/sG_5ZmpR3zo

40. **friend and CNN anchor:** CNN's Chris Cuomo, who was in isolation after testing positive for coronavirus, outlined the intense
symptoms with Dr. Sanjay Gupta, CNN Business, April 2, 2020,
https://www.cnn.com/videos/media/2020/04/02/chris-cuo-
mo-coronavirus-diagnosis-rigors-oxygen-gupta-cpt-vpx.cnn

41. **"I worry it will":** Clarissa Ward in conversation with Ramita
Navai at the Frontline Club London, October 29, 2020, https://
www.youtube.com/watch?v=-jDIbe3Y8lY

42. **courts in Ukraine:** interview with Natalia Sedletska,
December 21, 2020.

43. **Spain-based online newspaper:** *Spanish News Startup El Español
Carves out a New Digital Space While Competing With Legacy
Media,* Newman Lab, October 29, 2015, https://www.niemanlab.
org/2015/10/spanish-news-startup-el-espanol-carves-out-a-new-
digital-space-while-competing-with-legacy-media/

44. **amid the punishing lockdowns:** *El Español Exceeded 20 million
Readers on a Monthly Basis: Record Growth of 34% in 2020,* The
Canadian, January 4, 2021, https://thecanadian.news/2021/01/04/
el-espanol-exceeded-20-million-readers-on-a-monthly-basis-re-
cord-growth-of-34-in-2020/

45. **Young Turks:** *The Young Turks Expand Reporting Unit
Through $2 Million Crowdsource Fundraising Campaign,* TYT
press release, May 15, 2017, https://legacy.tyt.com/2017/05/18/
tyt-reaches-2-million-in-fundraising-campaign/

46. **impressive 200 million:** in January 2021, Tubular,
https://tubularlabs.com/creator/vwolhPKC79/
The-Young-Turks?tab=summary

47. **"depend on subscribers:** *Spanish News Startup El Español Carves out a New Digital Space While Competing With Legacy Media,* Newman Lab, October 29, 2015, https://www.niemanlab.org/2015/10/spanish-news-startup-el-espanol-carves-out-a-new-digital-space-while-competing-with-legacy-media/

48. **Dutch/English-language:** *How The Correspondent Exceeded its $2.5 Million Crowdfunding Goal,* The Lenfest Institute, January 17, 2019, https://www.lenfestinstitute.org/solution-set/how-the-correspondent-exceeded-its-2-5-million-crowdfunding-goal/

49. **farewell letter:** *The Correspondent will stop publishing on 1 January 2021. We'd like to thank our members for their support,* The Correspondent, December 10, 2020, https://thecorrespondent.com/834/the-correspondent-will-stop-publishing-on-1-january-2021-wed-like-to-thank-our-members-for-their-support/12825252-8c4236ca

50. **high net-worth:** interview with Fuller project's Xandie Scharff on Global Impact podcast, March 12, 2021, https://anchor.fm/michael-bociurkiw/episodes/S3-E5-In-Conversation-With-Xanthe-Scharff-esd351

51. **Jeff Bezos:** The founder of Amazon purchased The Washington Post for US$250 million in 2013, which is about half of what he paid for his 127m superyacht. See: *Jeff Bezos and the Secretive World of Superyachts,* BBC, May 14, 2021, https://www.bbc.com/news/world-us-canada-57079327. *Why Jeff Bezos Bought The Washington Post,* Stephanie Denning, Forbes, September 19, 2018, https://www.forbes.com/sites/stephaniedenning/2018/09/19/why-jeff-bezos-bought-the-washington-post/?sh=7206ed083aab

52. **"where things are going":** *Doubling Down on the Future,* Andreessen Horowitz blog post, by Margit Wennmachers, January 25, 2021, https://a16z.com/2021/01/25/doubling-down-marketing-update-new-media/

53. **"addiction-maximising feeds":** blog post by Substack Inc. co-founder Hamish McKenzie, January 4, 2021, https://blog.substack.com/p/welcome-facebook-and-twitter-seriously

54. **venture capitalist Peter Thiel:** *Peter Thiel Reportedly Looking Into Launching a Fox News Competitor,* The Verge, January 3, 2018, https://www.theverge.com/2018/1/3/16847508/peter-thiel-fox-news-competitor-cable-network-roger-ailes-trump

55. **New York-based hedge fund:** *Tribune Shareholders Vote to Sell Legendary Chain of Newspapers to a Hedge Fund, Washington Post,* May 21, 2021, https://www.washingtonpost.com/media/2021/05/21/tribune-sale-alden-hedge-fund/

56. **setting aside US$100 million:** *Facebook Invests Additional $100 Million to Support News Industry During the Coronavirus Crisis,* Facebook blog post by Campbell Brown, March 30, 2020, https://www.facebook.com/journalismproject/coronavirus-update-news-industry-support

57. **Zuckerberg:** *Facebook is Working on a Newsletter Tool for Freelancers and Independent Writers, The New York Times Reports,* Business Insider, January 28, 2021, https://www.businessinsider.com/facebook-is-working-on-a-newsletter-service-nyt-2021-1

58. **not to be outdone:** *Twitter Acquiring Newsletter Publishing Company Revue,* Axios, January 26, 2021, https://www.axios.com/twitter-newsletter-publishing-revue-8a74f20d-61c9-4095-9b3c-202c3b3fe77c.html?utm_source=twitter&utm_medium=social&utm_campaign=organic&utm_content=1100\

59. **declared bankruptcy:** *Too Much, Too Soon,* Forbes, October 20, 1997, https://www.forbes.com/forbes/1997/1020/6009052a.html?sh=560fd09026dd

60. **Asia Times still survives:** https://asiatimes.com/*Asia Times* is now run out of Hong Kong as an online publication in English and simplified Chinese. One of its columnists, identified as Pepe Escobar, is a Brazilian journalist who also comments for state-owned Russia Today and Iran's Press TV.

Manufactured by Amazon.ca
Bolton, ON

19727644R00090